STUDY GUIDE for

Discovering Computers 2003

Concepts for a Digital World

Web and XP Enhanced

Sabrina Wheatley
695-6116

Gary B. Shelly
Thomas J. Cashman
Tim J. Walker

THOMSON
COURSE TECHNOLOGY

COURSE TECHNOLOGY
25 THOMSON PLACE
BOSTON MA 02210

SHELLY CASHMAN SERIES®

Australia • Canada • Denmark • Japan • Mexico • New Zealand • Philippines • Puerto Rico • Singapore
South Africa • Spain • United Kingdom • United States

THOMSON

COURSE TECHNOLOGY

Asia (excluding Japan)
Thomson Learning
60 Albert Street, #15-01
Albert Complex
Singapore 189969

Japan
Thomson Learning
Palaceside Building 5F
1-1-1 Hitotsubashi, Chiyoda-ku
Tokyo 100 0003 Japan

Australia/New Zealand
Nelson/Thomson Learning
102 Dodds Street
South Melbourne, Victoria 3205
Australia

Latin America
Thomson Learning
Seneca, 53
Colonia Polanco
11560 Mexico D.F. Mexico

South Africa
Thomson Learning
Zonnebloem Building,
Constantia Square
526 Sixteenth Road
P.O. Box 2459
Halfway House, 1685
South Africa

Canada
Nelson/Thomson Learning
1120 Birchmount Road
Scarborough, Ontario
Canada M1K 5G4

UK/Europe/Middle East
Thomson Learning
Berkshire House
168-173 High Holborn
London, WC1V 7AA United Kingdom

Spain
Thomson Learning
Calle Magallanes, 25
28015-MADRID
ESPANA

For more information, contact Course Technology, 25 Thomson Place, Boston, MA 02210.

Or visit our Internet site at www.course.com

ISBN 0-7895-6537-4

1 2 3 4 5 6 7 8 9 10 BC 06 05 04 03 02

DISCOVERING COMPUTERS 2003

CONCEPTS FOR A DIGITAL WORLD

WEB AND XP ENHANCED

STUDY GUIDE

CONTENTS

PREFACE

This Study Guide is intended as a supplement to *Discovering Computers 2003: Concepts for a Digital World, Web and XP Enhanced* by Gary Shelly, Thomas Cashman, and Misty Vermaat. A variety of learning activities are provided in a format that is easy to follow and helps students recall, review, and master introductory computer concepts. Each chapter in the Study Guide includes:

- A **Chapter Overview** summarizing the chapter's content that helps students recollect the general character of the concepts presented.
- **Chapter Objectives** specifying the goals students should have achieved after finishing the chapter.
- A **Chapter Outline** designed to be completed by the students, helping them to identify, organize, and recognize the relationships between important concepts.
- A **Self Test** that reviews the material in the chapter through Matching, True/False, Multiple Choice, Fill in the Blanks, and Complete the Table questions.
- **Things to Think About**, which consists of questions formulated to help students develop a deeper understanding of the information in the chapter.
- A **Puzzle** that provides an entertaining approach to reviewing important terms and concepts.
- **Self Test Answers** and a **Puzzle Answer** that students can use to assess their mastery of the subject matter.

In addition to the activities in each chapter, the Study Guide also offers a **To the Student** section that provides tips on using the textbook effectively, attending class, preparing for and taking tests, and using this Study Guide.

Acknowledgments

The Shelly Cashman Series would not be the leading computer education series without the contributions of outstanding publishing professionals. First, and foremost, among them is Becky Herrington, director of production and designer. She is the heart and soul of the Shelly Cashman Series, and it is only through her leadership, dedication, and tireless efforts that superior products are made possible.

Under Becky's direction, the following individuals made significant contributions to these books: Doug Cowley, production manager; Ginny Harvey, series specialist and developmental editor; Ken Russo, senior Web and graphic designer; Mike Bodnar, associate production manager; Mark Norton, technical analyst; Michelle French, Christy Otten, and Stephanie Nance, graphic artists; Jeanne Black and Betty Hopkins, Quark XPress compositors; Lyn Markowicz, Nancy Lamm, and Kim Kosmatka, copyeditors/proofreaders; Cristina Haley, indexer; Abby Reip, photo researcher; and William Vermaat, researcher and photographer.

Finally, we would like to thank Richard Keaveny, associate publisher; Cheryl Ouellette, managing editor; Jim Quasney, series consulting editor; Alexandra Arnold, product manager; Erin Runyon, associate product manager; Marc Ouellette, Web product manager; Kate McAllister; marketing manager; and Reed Cotter, editorial assistant.

Gary B. Shelly
Thomas J. Cashman
Timothy J. Walker

To the Student

Would you like to be promised success in this course? Your textbook, *Discovering Computers 2003: Concepts for a Digital World*, can be a source of the knowledge you need to succeed. Unfortunately, no textbook alone can guarantee understanding of the subject matter; genuine understanding depends to a great extent on how hard you are willing to work. Other available resources, however, can *help* you to get the most out of this course. That is the intent of this Study Guide.

What follows are tips on using the textbook, attending class, preparing for and taking tests, and utilizing this Study Guide. Most of the tips in the first three areas not only will help to improve your performance in this course, they also can be applied to many of your other college classes. The tips in the last area are designed to explain how this Study Guide can enhance your mastery of the material in *Discovering Computers 2003: Concepts for a Digital World.*

🕮 Using the Textbook

The textbook is one of your most important tools for building a solid foundation in the subject matter. To use your textbook most effectively, follow these guidelines:

Survey the whole text first. The table of contents supplies an overview of the topics covered. The preface explains the textbook's objectives and features. Notice how chapters are organized, the way key terms and concepts are indicated, how illustrations and tables are used, and the types of exercises that conclude each chapter. Look for special features interspersed throughout the book and use the index to clarify information.

Start by skimming the chapter. Read the chapter introduction, which gives you an idea of the chapter's relevance, and study the chapter objectives, which indicate what you are expected to learn. Next, browse the chapter. Look at the section headings to get a feeling for how sections are related to each other. Note bold text — these terms are important. Primary Terms are shown in **bold black characters** and include terms commonly used in the computer industry and in advertisements, or terms that identify a major category. Secondary Terms are shown in **bold blue-gray characters** and include terms primarily used by IT professionals and other technical people, terms that identify subcategories, or terms that are discussed in more depth in a later chapter. Finally, read the Chapter Summary at the end of the chapter. The summary restates, in broad terms, the major concepts and conclusions offered in the chapter.

Carefully read the entire chapter. Some instructors prefer that you only skim a chapter before class, and then do a detailed reading after their lecture. Other instructors want you to read the chapter thoroughly before class. When you read through the text, make sure you understand all of the key terms and concepts. Pay particular attention to illustrations (photographs, diagrams, and tables) and their captions; often, they can help clarify ideas in the text. Examine the boxed write-ups interspersed throughout the chapter (Issue, Apply It!, Technology Trailblazer, Company on the Cutting Edge) and use the Web Links in the margins to obtain additional information. Write in your book: highlight important points, note relationships, and jot questions. Read the E-Revolution section that concludes each chapter in *Discovering Computers 2003: Concepts for a Digital World.* This section describes various resources that are available on the World Wide Web. Carefully examine the review material (In Summary) and list of important words (Key Terms). If there is anything you do not remember or understand, go back and re-read the relevant sections. Do the exercises that deal specifically with the content of the chapter (Checkpoint). Finally, complete any additional exercises (Learn It Online, In the Lab, or Web Work) that your instructor may assign.

Attending Class

Attending class is a key ingredient to success in a course. Simply showing up, however, is not enough. To get the most out of class, follow these guidelines:

Arrive early and prepared. Sit close enough to the front of the room to hear well and see any visual materials, such as slides or transparencies, clearly. Have any necessary supplies, such as a notebook and writing implement or a notebook computer, and your textbook. Be ready to start when your instructor begins.

Take notes. For most people, taking notes is essential to later recall the material presented in class. Note-taking styles vary: some people simply jot down keywords and concepts, while others prefer to write more detailed accounts. The important thing is that the style you adopt works for you. If, when you later consult your notes, you find they do little to help you remember the subject of the lecture, perhaps you should try to be more comprehensive. On the other hand, if you find that in taking notes you frequently fall behind your instructor, try to be briefer. Review your notes as soon as possible after class.

Do not hesitate to ask questions. Often, people are afraid to ask questions because they think they will appear foolish. In reality, asking good questions is a sign of intelligence; after all, you have to be insightful enough to realize something is unclear. Keep in mind that frequently your classmates have the same questions you do. Good questions not only help to clarify difficult topics, they also increase the depth of your understanding by suggesting relationships between ideas or establishing the significance of concepts. Learn the best time to ask questions. In small classes, sometimes it is possible to ask questions during instruction. In a larger setting, it may be best to approach your instructor after class or to make an appointment. If you feel really lost, your instructor may be able to recommend a peer tutor or an academic counseling service to help you.

Preparing for and Taking Tests

Tests are an opportunity for you to demonstrate how much you have learned. Some strategies are certain to improve performance on tests. To do your best on a test, follow these guidelines:

Find out as much as you can about the test. Ask your instructor what material will be covered, what types of questions will be used, how much time you will have, and what supplies you will need (pencil or pen, paper or bluebook, perhaps even notes or a textbook if it is an open-book test). You will be more likely to do your best work if there are no surprises. Occasionally, copies of previous tests are available from the department or school library. These are invaluable aids in test preparation.

Use your resources wisely. Start studying by reviewing your notes and, in *Discovering Computers 2003: Concepts for a Digital World*, the In Summary section at the end of each chapter. Review carefully and attempt to anticipate some of the questions that may be asked. Re-read the sections in your textbook on topics you are not sure of or that seem especially important. Try to really comprehend, and not merely memorize, the material. If you truly understand a concept, you will be able to answer any question, no matter what type or how it is worded. Understanding often makes remembering easier, too; for example, if you know that an ink-jet printer works by spraying dots of ink on a page, it is simple to recall that ink-jet printer resolution is measured in dots per inch (dpi). When memorizing is necessary, use whatever technique works (memory tricks, verbal repetition, flash cards, and so on).

Avoid cramming. To prepare for an athletic contest, you would not practice for twelve straight hours before the event. In the same way, you should not expect to do well on a test by spending the entire night before it cramming. When you cram, facts become easily confused, and anything you do keep straight probably will be remembered only for a short time. It also is difficult to recognize how concepts are related, which can be an important factor in successful test taking. Try to study in increments over a period of time. Use the night before the test to do a general review of the pertinent material, concentrating on what seems most difficult. Then, get a good night's sleep so you are well rested and at your best when it is time for the test.

Take time to look through the test. Arrive early enough at the test site to get properly settled. Listen for any special instructions that might be given. Skim the entire test before you start. Read the directions carefully; you may not have to answer every question, or you may be asked to answer questions in a certain way. Determine the worth of each part, the parts you think can be done most quickly, and the parts you believe will take the longest to complete. Use your assessment to budget your time.

Answer the questions you are sure of first. As you work through the test, read each question carefully and answer the easier ones first. If you are not certain of an answer, skip that question for now. This guarantees that you get the maximum number of "sure" points and reduces worry about time when later dealing with the more difficult questions. Occasionally, you will find that the information you needed to answer one of the questions you skipped can be found elsewhere in the test. Other times, you will suddenly remember what you need to answer a question you skipped as you are dealing with another part of the test.

Use common sense. Most questions have logical answers. While these answers often require specific knowledge of the subject matter, sometimes it is possible to determine a correct answer with a general understanding and a little common sense. As you work through a test, and when you go back over the test after you are finished, make sure all your answers are reasonable. Do not change an answer, however, unless you are sure your first answer was wrong. If incorrect answers are not penalized any more than having no answer at all, it is better to try a logical guess than to leave an answer blank. But, if you are penalized for incorrect answers (for example, if your final score is the number of correct answers minus the number of incorrect answers), you will have to decide whether or not to answer a question based on how confident you are of your guess.

✎ Using this Study Guide

The purpose of this Study Guide is to further your understanding of the concepts presented in *Discovering Computers 2003: Concepts for a Digital World.* Each Study Guide chapter should be completed *after* you have finished the corresponding chapter in the book. The Study Guide chapters are divided into sections, each of which has a specific purpose:

Chapter Overview This is a brief summary of the chapter's content. The Chapter Overview helps you recall the general nature of the information in the chapter.

Chapter Objectives This is a list of the same objectives that introduce the chapter in the book. After completing the chapter, review the Chapter Objectives to determine how many of them you have met. If you have not reached an objective, go back and review the appropriate material or your notes.

Chapter Outline This is a partially completed outline of the chapter with page numbers where topics can be found. The Chapter Outline is designed to help you review the material and to assist you in organizing and seeing the relationships between concepts. Complete the outline in as much depth as you feel necessary. There is no one "right answer" in the Chapter Outline. Because your completions should be meaningful to *you*, they may be different from a classmate's. You can refer directly to the text as you work through the outline while re-reading the chapter, or you can fill in the outline on your own and then use the text to check the information you have supplied.

Self Test This is a tool you can use to evaluate your mastery of the chapter. The Self Test consists of five different types of questions: matching, true/false, multiple choice, fill in the blanks, and complete the table. Take the Self Test without referring to your textbook or notes. Leave any answer you are unsure of blank or, if you prefer, guess at the answer but indicate you were unsure by placing a question mark (?) after your response. When you have finished, check your work against the Self Test Answers at the end of the Study Guide chapter. Each answer is accompanied by the page number in *Discovering Computers 2003: Concepts for a Digital World* where the answer can be found. Review any solution that was incorrect or any reply that was uncertain.

Things to Think About These questions are meant to help you better grasp the information in each chapter. Because specific answers to the Things to Think About questions will vary, no solutions are given. The true purpose of these questions is to get you to contemplate the "why" behind concepts, thus encouraging you to gain a greater understanding of the ideas, their connections, and their significance.

Puzzle This activity is designed to review important terms in an entertaining fashion. The Puzzle in each chapter is one of four types: a word search puzzle, a crossword puzzle, a puzzle in which words must be placed in a grid, or a puzzle involving words written in code. Every puzzle offers definitions or descriptions and asks you to supply the associated term. The solution to each puzzle is given.

DISCOVERING COMPUTERS 2003

STUDY GUIDE

CHAPTER 1

Introduction to Computers

Chapter Overview

This chapter introduces basic computer concepts such as what a computer is, how it works, and what makes it a powerful tool. You also learn about the components of a computer. Next, the chapter discusses computer software, networks, and the Internet. The many different categories of computers and computer users also are presented. This chapter is an overview. Many of the terms and concepts introduced are discussed further in later chapters.

Chapter Objectives

After completing this chapter, you should be able to:

- Explain the importance of computer literacy
- Define the term computer
- Identify the components of a computer
- Explain why a computer is a powerful tool
- Differentiate among the various types of software
- Explain the purpose of a network
- Discuss the uses of the Internet and the World Wide Web
- Describe the categories of computers and their uses
- Identify the various types of computer users
- Understand how a user can be a Web publisher

Chapter Outline

I. The digital revolution [p. 1.02]

The digital revolution is upon us, as computers extend into more facets of daily living. Being computer literate means ________________________________

____

II. What is a computer? [p. 1.04]

A computer is ________________________________

____

____

A. Data and information [p. 1.04]

- Data is ____

  ____

- Information is ____

  ____

Computers process data to create information.

A user is ____

- Hardware is ____

  ____

- Software is ____

  ____

B. Information processing cycle [p. 1.05]

Input is ____

Output is ____

Computers process input (______________) into output (______________).

Storage is ____

The information processing cycle is ____

____

III. The components of a computer [p. 1.05]

A. Input devices [p. 1.05]

An input device is ____

____

Common input devices: ____

____

B. Output devices [p. 1.06]

An output device is ____

____

Common output devices: ____

C. System unit [p. 1.06]

The system unit is ____

____

The system unit circuitry usually is part of or is connected to the motherboard.

Two main components on the motherboard are the CPU and memory.

- The central processing unit (CPU) is ____

  ____

- Memory is ____

  ____

D. Storage devices [p. 1.06]

A storage device records and retrieves ______________________________

____

A storage medium is the physical material on which a computer keeps the data, instructions, and information.

Common storage devices: ______________________________

____

E. Communications devices [p. 1.08]

Communications devices enable ______________________________

____

Communications devices: ______________________________

IV. Why is a computer so powerful? [p. 1.08]

A computer's power is derived from its:

A. Speed [p. 1.08]

____

B. Reliability [p. 1.09]

____

C. Accuracy [p. 1.09]

____

The phrase garbage in, garbage out (GIGO) points out ________________

____

D. Storage [p. 1.09]

____

E. Communications [p. 1.09]

____

V. Computer software [p. 1.10]

A computer program is ____

____

With some programs, you must install the program instructions on the computer's hard disk. When the computer executes the program, the instructions are loaded from the hard disk into the computer's memory.

Two types of software are system software and application software.

A. System software [p. 1.12]

System software consists ____

____

Two types of system software are the operating system and utility programs.

1. Operating system [p. 1.12]

   An operating system (OS) is ________________________________

   ____

2. Utility programs [p. 1.12]

   A utility program is ______________________________________

   ____

3. User interface [p. 1.12]

   The user interface controls how you enter data and instructions and how information displays on the screen.

   With a graphical user interface (GUI) you interact ________________

   ____

B. Application software [p. 1.13]

Application software consists ____________________________________

____

Popular application software includes ______________________________

____

Sources of application software:

1. Packaged software [p. 1.13]

   Packaged software is ______________________________________

   ____

2. Custom software [p. 1.14]

   Custom software is ____

   ____

3. Freeware, public-domain software, and shareware [p. 1.14]

   - Freeware is ____

     ____

   - Public-domain software is _________________________________

     ____

   - Shareware is ____

     ____

4. Application service provider [p. 1.15]
   An application service provider is ______________________________

   ____

C. Software development [p. 1.15]
   A computer programmer is ______________________________

   ____

   A systems analyst designs ______________________________

   ____

VI. Networks and the Internet [p. 1.16]
A network is ____

____

The Internet is ____

____

People use the Internet to ______________________________

____

VII. Categories of computers [p. 1.19]
Computer categories are based on size, speed, processing capabilities, and price.
The six major categories of computers are:

- ______________________
- ______________________
- ______________________
- ______________________
- ______________________
- ______________________

VIII. Personal computers [p. 1.19]
A personal computer is ______________________________

____

Two popular series of personal computers are the PC and the Apple Macintosh.
Major categories of personal computers:

A. Desktop computers [p. 1.20]
   A desktop computer is ______________________________

   ____

   A tower model has ______________________________

   ____

   An all-in-one computer is ______________________________

   ____

   A workstation is ______________________________

   ____

B. Notebook computers [p. 1.22]
A notebook computer is ____

____

IX. Handheld computers [p. 1.23]
A handheld computer is ____

____

A PDA (personal digital assistant) is ____

____

Some handheld computers are Web-enabled. Other Web-enabled devices:

- A Web-enabled cellular telephone allows ____

  ____

- A Web-enabled pager is ____

  ____

X. Internet appliances [p. 1.24]
An Internet appliance is ____

____

XI. Mid-range servers [p. 1.25]
A mid-range server is ____

____

XII. Mainframes [p. 1.26]
A mainframe is ____

____

XIII. Supercomputers [p. 1.26]
A supercomputer is ____

____

XIV. Elements of an information system [p. 1.27]
An information system is comprised ____

____

For an information system to be successful, all of these elements must be present and work together.

XV. Examples of computer usage [p. 1.28]
Different categories of users rely on computers for a variety of purposes.

A. Home user [p. 1.29]

____

____

____

____

The digital divide is ______________________________

____

B. Small office/home office user [p. 1.31]

____

____

____

____

E-commerce is ______________________________

C. Mobile user [p. 1.32]

____

____

____

____

D. Large business user [p. 1.33]

____

____

____

____

Telecommuting is ______________________________

E. Power user [p. 1.35]

____

____

____

____

Multimedia combines ______________________________

XVI. Computer user as a Web publisher [p. 1.36]

In addition to being a recipient of information on the Internet, users can *provide* information to other connected users around the world.

Publishing a Web page is ______________________________

____

Users publish Web pages for a variety of reasons:

- ______________________________
- ______________________________
- ______________________________
- ______________________________

Photo communities are ______________________________

____

Self Test

Matching

1. ____ input device
2. ____ output device
3. ____ system unit
4. ____ storage device
5. ____ communications device
6. ____ packaged software
7. ____ custom software
8. ____ freeware
9. ____ public-domain software
10. ____ shareware

a. copyrighted retail software that meets the needs of a wide variety of users

b. allows a user to enter data and instructions into a computer

c. writes the instructions necessary to process data into information

d. tailor-made programs developed at a user's request to perform specific functions

e. free software donated for public use with no copyright restrictions

f. box-like case that protects a computer's internal electronic components from damage

g. enables computer users to exchange items with another computer

h. collection of computers connected together via telephone lines, modems, or other means

i. copyrighted software provided by an individual or company at no cost

j. records and retrieves items to and from a medium

k. any component that can convey information to a user

l. copyrighted software distributed free for a trial period

True/False

____ 1. Through computers, society has access to information from all around the globe.

____ 2. Without software, most hardware is useless; hardware needs instructions from software to process data into information.

____ 3. A mouse contains keys that allow you to type letters of the alphabet, numbers, spaces, punctuation marks, and other symbols.

____ 4. A peripheral is any internal device that resides inside the system unit.

____ 5. Storage differs from memory in that it holds items only temporarily while the processor interprets and executes them, whereas memory can hold items permanently.

____ 6. When two or more computers are connected together via communications media and devices, they form a network.

____ 7. A computer program might load into memory from the hard disk each time you execute the program.

____ 8. Hardware is the key to productive use of computers.

____ 9. Most users connect to the Internet in one of two ways: through an Internet service provider or through an online service provider.

____ 10. Few SOHO (small office/home office) computer users communicate with each other through e-mail.

Multiple Choice

____ 1. How does information differ from data?
   a. information is a collection of raw unprocessed facts
   b. information can include words, numbers, images, and sounds
   c. information is organized, meaningful, and useful
   d. information is processed to produce data

____ 2. What are examples of input devices?
   a. the keyboard and the mouse
   b. the central processing unit (CPU) and memory
   c. the printer and the monitor
   d. all of the above

____ 3. What component is *not* considered a peripheral?
   a. the keyboard
   b. the CPU
   c. a microphone
   d. a monitor

____ 4. Why is a computer so powerful?
   a. because it can perform the information processing cycle operations with amazing speed, reliability, and accuracy
   b. because it can store huge amounts of data
   c. because it can communicate with other computers
   d. all of the above

____ 5. Word processing, spreadsheet, database, and presentation graphics software are what type of software?
   a. system software
   b. operating systems
   c. application software
   d. utility programs

____ 6. Instead of installing software on their computer, some people run programs from the Internet and opt to use what for their software needs?
   a. an Internet service provider (ISP)
   b. an online service provider (OSP)
   c. an application service provider (ASP)
   d. an executable service provider (ESP)

____ 7. Why do people use the Internet?
   a. to meet or converse with people around the world
   b. to access sources of entertainment and leisure
   c. to shop for goods and services
   d. all of the above

____ 8. What is a workstation?
   a. a large, expensive, very powerful computer that can handle hundreds or thousands of connected users simultaneously
   b. a mainframe computer powerful enough to function as a server on a network
   c. an expensive, powerful desktop computer designed for work that requires intense calculations and graphics capabilities
   d. a popular type of handheld computer that often supports personal information management applications

____ 9. What is the fastest, most powerful category of computers – and the most expensive?
   a. personal computers
   b. minicomputers
   c. mainframe computers
   d. supercomputers

____ 10. A local law practice, accounting firm, travel agency, and florist are examples of what type of computer user?
   a. mobile user
   b. small office/home office user
   c. power user
   d. large business user

Fill in the Blanks

1. A(n) ____________________ is someone that communicates with a computer or employs the information it generates.
2. During processing, a computer processor places instructions to be executed and data needed by those instructions into ____________________.
3. A graphical user interface uses visual images such as ____________________ that represent programs, instructions, or some other object.
4. You are considered ____________________ when your computer connects to a network.

5. The world's largest network is the ____________________, a worldwide collection of networks that links together millions of computers.
6. A(n) ____________________ computer can perform the information processing cycle operations by itself without being connected to a network.
7. A(n) ____________________ is a computer that manages the resources on a network.
8. Users typically access a mid-range server via a(n) ____________________, which is a device with a monitor and a keyboard.
9. Some Web sites use a(n) ____________________, which is a video camera with output that can be displayed on a Web page.
10. A(n) ____________________ is a freestanding computer, usually with a touch screen that serves as an input device.

Complete the Table

CATEGORIES OF COMPUTERS

Category	Physical size	Number of simultaneously connected users	General price range
Personal computer (desktop or notebook)	Fits on a desk or on your lap	____________________ ____________________	____________________ ____________________
____________________	Fits in your hand	____________________ ____________________	Several hundred dollars or less
Internet appliance	__________ __________	Usually one	____________________ ____________________
____________________	__________ __________	Two to thousands	$5,000 to $850,000
Mainframe	Partial to full room	____________________ ____________________	____________________ ____________________
____________________	__________ __________	Hundreds to thousands	Several million dollars and up

Things to Think About

1. Do the four operations in the information processing cycle (input, process, output, and storage) always have to be performed in order? Why or why not?
2. Why is each component of a computer system (input devices, system unit, output devices, secondary storage devices) important?
3. Why is software the key to productive use of computers?
4. Why do mobile users often have notebook computers equipped with a modem?

Puzzle

All of the words described below appear in the puzzle. Words may be either forward or backward, across, up and down, or diagonal. Circle each word as you find it.

Introduction to Computers

						P	E						
						D	U						
						A	S						
		S	T	H		T	E		J	E	K		
	H	A	R	D	W	A	R	E	V	R	E	S	
G	S	R	E	T	U	P	M	O	C	I	N	I	M
U	T	B	T	I	N	U	M	E	T	S	Y	S	E
I	E	M	U	L	T	I	M	E	D	I	A	G	M
N	N	C	P	U	E	R	A	W	E	E	R	F	O
P	R	F	M	A	I	N	F	R	A	M	E	J	R
U	E	W	O	R	K	S	T	A	T	I	O	N	Y
T	T	K	C	R	E	G	A	R	O	T	S	T	A
	N	S	R	E	M	M	A	R	G	O	R	P	
	I	O	E	S	H	A	R	E	W	A	R	E	
		I	P	S	O	F	T	W	A	R	E		
		K	U	T	E	R	M	I	N	A	L		
			S	T	U	P	T	U	O	A			
			W	K	R	O	W	T	E	N			
					N	O	C	I					

Interprets and carries out instructions

Allows interaction using visual images

Worldwide collection of networks

PC designed to connect to a network

Computer that can perform all information processing activities

Often supports PIM applications

Process data into information

Collection of unorganized facts

Software provided at no cost to a user

Electronic and mechanical equipment

Small image that represents a program

Organized, meaningful, useful data

Data entered into a computer

Freestanding computer, usually with a touch screen

Can handle thousands of connected users

Temporarily holds data and instructions

More powerful than a workstation

Combines text, graphics, sound, video, and other elements

Collection of connected computers

Result of processing data

People who write computer instructions

Manages network resources

Software distributed free for a trial period

Instructions to process data into information

Where data is held for future use

Fastest, most powerful computer

Box-like case housing computer circuitry

Device with a monitor and a keyboard

Communicates with a computer or uses the information it generates

Expensive and powerful desktop computer

Self Test Answers

Matching

1. *b* [p. 1.05]
2. *k* [p. 1.06]
3. *f* [p. 1.06]
4. *j* [p. 1.07]
5. *g* [p. 1.08]
6. *a* [p. 1.13]
7. *d* [p. 1.14]
8. *i* [p. 1.14]
9. *e* [p. 1.14]
10. *l* [p. 1.14]

True/False

1. *T* [p. 1.03]
2. *T* [p. 1.04]
3. *F* [p. 1.05]
4. *F* [p. 1.06]
5. *F* [p. 1.06]
6. *T* [p. 1.10]
7. *T* [p. 1.10]
8. *F* [p. 1.11]
9. *T* [p. 1.18]
10. *F* [p. 1.31]

Multiple Choice

1. *c* [p. 1.04]
2. *a* [p. 1.05]
3. *b* [p. 1.06]
4. *d* [p. 1.08]
5. *c* [p. 1.13]
6. *c* [p. 1.15]
7. *d* [p. 1.17]
8. *c* [p. 1.21]
9. *d* [p. 1.26]
10. *b* [p. 1.31]

Fill in the Blanks

1. *user* [p. 1.04]
2. *memory* [p. 1.06]
3. *icons* [p. 1.12]
4. *online* [p. 1.16]
5. *Internet* [p. 1.17]
6. *stand-alone* [p. 1.21]
7. *server* [p. 1.21]
8. *terminal* [p. 1.25]
9. *Web cam* [p. 1.31]
10. *kiosk* [p. 1.34]

Complete the Table

CATEGORIES OF COMPUTERS

Category	Physical size	Number of simultaneously connected users	General price range
Personal computer (desktop or notebook)	Fits on a desk or on your lap	*Usually one, or many networked*	*Several thousand dollars or less*
Handheld computer	Fits in your hand	*Usually one*	Several hundred dollars or less
Internet appliance	*Fits on a countertop*	Usually one	*Several hundred dollars or less*
Mid-range server	*Small cabinet*	Two to thousands	$5,000 to $850,000
Mainframe	Partial to full room	*Hundreds to thousands*	*$300,000 to several million dollars*
Supercomputer	*Full room*	Hundreds to thousands	Several million dollars and up

Things to Think About

Answers will vary.

Puzzle Answer

Introduction to Computers

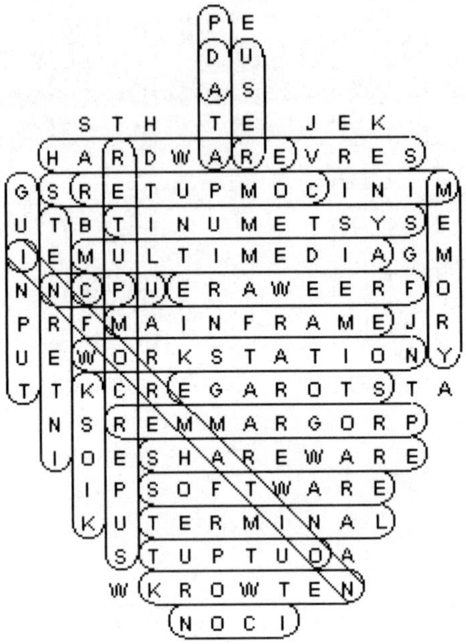

DISCOVERING COMPUTERS 2003

STUDY GUIDE

CHAPTER 2

The Internet and World Wide Web

Chapter Overview

This chapter presents the history and structure of the Internet. It describes at length the World Wide Web, including topics such as browsing, navigating, e-commerce, and Web publishing. It also introduced other services available on the Internet, such as e-mail, FTP, newsgroups and message boards, chat rooms, and instant messaging. Finally, the chapter lists rules of netiquette.

Chapter Objectives

After completing this chapter, you should be able to:

- Describe how the Internet works
- Understand ways to access the Internet
- Identify a URL
- Search for information on the Web
- Describe the types of Web pages
- Recognize how Web pages use graphics, animation, audio, video, and virtual reality
- Define Webcasting
- Describe the uses of electronic commerce (e-commerce)
- Identify the tools required for Web publishing
- Explain how e-mail, FTP, newsgroups and message boards, mailing lists, chat rooms, and instant messaging work
- Identify the rules of netiquette

Chapter Outline

I. The Internet [p. 2.02]

A network is ______________________________

____

The Internet (or the Net) is ______________________________

____

____

____

Millions of people use the Internet to ______________________________

____

____

II. History of the Internet [p. 2.03]

In 1969, a network called ARPANET, developed by the Advanced Research Projects Agency, became functional, linking scientific and academic researchers in the United States.

In 1986, the National Science Foundation connected its network, called NSFnet, to ARPANET, a configuration that became known as the Internet.

Even as it grows, the Internet remains ______________________________

____

The World Wide Web Consortium (W3C) is ______________________________

____

Internet 2 (I2) is ______________________________

____

III. How the Internet works [p. 2.04]

Data sent over the Internet travels via networks and communications channels owned by many companies.

A. Service providers [p. 2.05]

An Internet service provider (ISP) is ______________________________

____

A point of presence (POP) is ______________________________

Types of ISPs:

- A regional ISP provides ______________________________

  ____

- A national ISP provides ______________________________

  ____

An online service supplies ______________________________

____

A wireless service provider (WSP) is ______________________________

____

B. Connecting to the Internet [p. 2.06]

Many personal computers connect to a local area network (LAN) that connects to a service provider through a leased, high-speed connection line leased from the local telephone company.

Dial-up access uses ______________________________

____

DSL (digital subscriber line) provides ______________________________

____

A cable modem provides ______________________________

____

C. How data travels the Internet [p. 2.06]

Computers connected to the Internet transfer data and information using servers and clients.

- A server is ______________________________

  ____

- A client is ______________________________

  ____

The Internet backbone is ______________________________

____

D. Internet addresses [p. 2.08]

An IP (Internet protocol) address is ______________________________

____

A domain name is ______________________________

A top-level domain (TLD) abbreviation identifies ______________________________

____

The Internet Corporation for Assigned Names and Numbers (ICANN) assigns

____

The domain name system (DNS) is ______________________________

____

IV. World Wide Web [p. 2.09]

The World Wide Web (WWW), or Web, consists ______________________________

____

A Web page is ______________________________

A Web site is ______________________________

A. Browsing the Web [p. 2.09]

A Web browser is ______________________________

____

A home page is ______________________________

Downloading is ____

____

A microbrowser is ____

____

B. Navigating Web pages [p. 2.11]

A hyperlink, or link is ____

____

Links allow you to obtain information in a nonlinear way; that is, by making associations between topics instead of moving sequentially through the topics.

Links can be identified by ____

____

To activate a link, you point ____

____

C. Using a URL [p. 2.12]

A URL (Uniform Resource Locator) is ____

____

If you know the URL of a Web page, you can type it into a text box at the top of the browser window to display the page.

Most Web page URLs begin with http://, which stands for hypertext transfer protocol, the communications standard used to transfer Web pages.

A Web server is ____

D. Searching for information on the Web [p. 2.14]

A search engine is ____

____

To find a Web page, you enter search text or keywords into the search engine's text box.

A spider is ____

A hit is ____

When a search engine displays a list of hits, you can click a link in the list to display the associated Web page.

E. Types of Web pages [p. 2.16]

There are six basic types of Web pages:

1. Portal Web page [p. 2.16]

   A portal Web page offers ____

   ____

A Web community is ______________________________

A Wireless portal is ______________________________

2. News Web page [p. 2.17]

A news Web page contains ______________________________

____

3. Informational Web page [p. 2.17]

An informational Web page contains ______________________________

____

4. Business/marketing Web page [p. 2.17]

A business/marketing Web page contains ______________________________

____

5. Advocacy Web page [p. 2.17]

An advocacy Web page contains ______________________________

____

6. Personal Web page [p. 2.17]

A personal Web page is ______________________________

____

F. Multimedia on the Web [p. 2.18]

Multimedia refers ______________________________

____

1. Graphics [p. 2.18]

A graphic is ______________________________

____

Common file formats for graphical images on the Web:

- A JPEG (Joint Photographic Experts Group) file is ______________

  ____
- A GIF (Graphics Interchange Format) file uses ______________

  ____

A thumbnail is ______________________________

2. Animation [p. 2.19]

Animation is ______________________________

____

An animated GIF uses ______________________________

____

3. Audio [p. 2.20]
   Audio is ______________________________

   ____

   MP3 is ______________________________
   An MP3 player is a portable device that plays MP3 files stored on CD.
   Streaming is ______________________________

   ____

   Streaming audio enables ______________________________

   ____

4. Video [p. 2.22]
   Video consists ______________________________

   ____

   The Motion Picture Experts Group (MPEG) defines a popular video compression standard.
   Streaming video allows ______________________________

   ____

5. Virtual reality [p. 2.22]
   Virtual reality (VR) is ______________________________

   ____

   A VR world is ______________________________
   VR often is ______________________________

   ____

G. Webcasting [p. 2.23]
   Pull technology relies ______________________________

   ____

   Using push technology, a server automatically downloads ______________________________

   ____

   Webcasting uses ______________________________

   ____

   Push technology allows you to view Web content offline, which means ______

   ____

H. Electronic commerce [p. 2.24]
   Electronic commerce (e-commerce) is ______________________________

   ____

   M-commerce (mobile commerce) identifies ______________________________

   ____

Types of e-commerce:

- Business-to-consumer (B-to-C or B2C) e-commerce consists ____________

  ____

  An electronic storefront contains ______________________

  ____

  A shopping cart allows ______________________________
- Consumer-to-consumer (C-to-C or C2C) e-commerce occurs ________

  ____
- Business-to-business (B-to-B or B2B) e-commerce occurs __________

  ____

I. Web publishing [p. 2.26]

Web publishing is ______________________________

____

Steps to Web publishing:

1. Planning a Web site [p. 2.26]

   Planning involves ______________________________

   ____
2. Analyzing and designing a Web site [p. 2.26]

   Analyzing and designing determines ______________

   ____

   A plug-in is ______________________________
3. Creating a Web site [p. 2.28]

   Creating, or Web page authoring, involves ____________

   ____

   Web page authoring software is ____________________

   ____

   HTML (hypertext markup language) is ______________

   ____
4. Deploying a Web site [p. 2.29]

   Deploying involves uploading, or copying, the Web site you have created to a Web server.

   Web hosting services provide ______________________

   ____

   A submission service is ______________________

   ____

5. Maintaining a Web site [p. 2.29]

   A Webmaster is ______________________________

   ____

V. Other Internet services [p. 2.29]

In addition to the World Wide Web, many other Internet services are used widely.

A. E-mail [p. 2.30]

E-mail (electronic mail) is ______________________________

____

Using an e-mail program, messages can be created, sent, received, forwarded, stored, printed, and deleted.

An e-mail address is ______________________________

____

- A user name (user-ID) is ______________________________

  ____

- A domain name is supplied by the service provider.

An address book contains ______________________________

A mailbox is ______________________________

A mail server is ______________________________

POP (Post Office Protocol) is ______________________________

____

B. FTP [p. 2.32]

FTP (File Transfer Protocol) is ______________________________

____

An FTP server is ______________________________

____

An FTP site is ______________________________

____

C. Newsgroups and message boards [p. 2.33]

A newsgroup is ______________________________

____

Usenet is ______________________________

A news server is ______________________________

A newsreader is a program used to participate in a newsgroup.

An article is ______________________________

____

A thread (threaded discussion) consists ______________________________

____

When you subscribe to a newsgroup, its location is ____________________

____

In a moderated newsgroup, the moderator reviews _____________________

____

A message board is ____

____

D. Mailing lists [p. 2.34]

A mailing list is ____

____

When you subscribe to a mailing list, you add your name and e-mail address to it; when you unsubscribe, you remove your name.

E. Chat rooms [p. 2.35]

A chat is ____

____

- Real time means ____

A chat room is ____

____

A chat client is ____

____

F. Instant messaging [p. 2.36]

Instant messaging (IM) is ______________________________________

____

An instant messenger is _______________________________________

____

VI. Netiquette [p. 2.37]

Netiquette is ____

____

Some rules of Netiquette:

Golden Rule: Treat ____

1. In e-mail, newsgroups, and chat rooms:
   - Keep messages brief.
   - Be careful when using ______________________________________
   - Be polite.

- Avoid sending or posting flames, which are ______________________________

  ____

- Avoid sending spam, which is ______________________________________

  ____

- Do not use all capital letters, which is the equivalent of SHOUTING!
- Use emoticons to express ____

  ____

  ____

- Use abbreviations and acronyms for common phrases.

  ____

  ____

- Clearly identify a spoiler, which is _______________________________

  ____

2. Read the FAQ (frequently asked questions) document.
3. Do not assume ____
4. Never read ____

Self Test

Matching

1. ____ Web browser
2. ____ search engine
3. ____ player
4. ____ plug-in
5. ____ Web page authoring software
6. ____ e-mail program
7. ____ FTP server
8. ____ newsreader
9. ____ chat client
10. ____ instant messenger

a. a computer that allows users to upload and download files using FTP

b. a software program used to access and view Web pages

c. a software program, included with most browsers, used to participate in a newsgroup

d. a software program that extends the capability of a browser

e. a software program used to store multiple Web pages at a single site

f. programs specifically designed to help you create Web pages

g. a software program used to create, send, receive, forward, store, print, and delete messages

h. a software program that stores personal data on a client computer

i. a software program that can play the audio in MP3 files on your computer

j. a software program installed onto the computer or device with which you use IM

k. a software program used to find Web sites, Web pages, and Internet files

l. a software program through which you connect to a chat server to start a chat session

True/False

____ 1. Although each network on the Internet is owned by a public or private organization, no single organization owns or controls the Internet.

____ 2. Due to their size, national ISPs usually offer fewer services and generally have a smaller technical support staff than regional ISPs.

____ 3. In general, the first portion of each IP (Internet protocol) address identifies the specific computer, and the last portion identifies the network.

____ 4. To remind you visually that you have visited a location or document, some browsers change the color of a text link after you click it.

____ 5. Newspapers and television and radio stations are some of the media that maintain news Web pages.

____ 6. Two of the more common formats for graphical images on the Web are MP3 and MPEG.

____ 7. To develop a Web page, you have to be a computer programmer; for the small business or home user, Web publishing is very difficult.

____ 8. When you receive an e-mail message, it is placed in your mailbox, which is a storage location residing on the computer that connects you to the Internet.

____ 9. Before you use a compressed file, you must compress it with a compression program.

____ 10. Some mailing lists are called LISTSERVs, named after a popular list software product.

Multiple Choice

____ 1. What group oversees research and sets standards and guidelines for many areas of the Internet?
   a. the Advanced Research Projects Agency (ARPA)
   b. the Uniform Resource Locator (URL)
   c. the Joint Photographic Experts Group (JPEG)
   d. the World Wide Web Consortium (W3C)

____ 2. In the URL http://www.nationalgeographic.com/travel/index.html, what is http://?
   a. the protocol
   b. the domain name
   c. the path
   d. the document name

____ 3. For what type of images does the GIF format work best?
   a. scanned photographs
   b. line drawings and simple cartoons
   c. multi-hued artwork
   d. images with smooth color variations

____ 4. What is a small version of a large graphical image you usually can click to display the full-sized image?
   a. a tag
   b. a marquee
   c. a thumbnail
   d. a player

____ 5. What is a VR world?
   a. an entire 3-D site that contains infinite space and depth
   b. a Web site that joins a group of people with similar interests
   c. a location on an Internet server that permits users to talk
   d. a Web site where you bid on an item being sold by someone else

____ 6. When you visit an online business through an electronic storefront, in what type of e-commerce are you participating?
a. business-to-consumer (B-to-C or B2C) e-commerce
b. consumer-to-consumer (C-to-C or C2C) e-commerce
c. business-to-business (B-to-B or B2B) e-commerce
d. consumer-to-business (C-to-B or C2B) e-commerce

____ 7. What companies provide storage for Web pages for a reasonable monthly fee?
a. Web page wizards
b. Web page publishers
c. Web browser facilitators
d. Web hosting services

____ 8. What communications technology is used to retrieve e-mail from a server?
a. SMTP (Simple Mail Transfer Protocol)
b. POP (Post Office Protocol)
c. HTTP (hypertext transfer protocol)
d. ISP (Internet service protocol)

____ 9. What is a previously entered newsgroup message called?
a. a spider
b. a crawler
c. a spoiler
d. an article

____ 10. Which of the following is *not* a rule of netiquette?
a. keep messages brief, using proper grammar and spelling
b. read the FAQ (frequently asked questions), if one exists
c. assume all material is accurate and up to date
d. be careful when using sarcasm and humor

Fill in the Blanks

1. On the Internet, your computer is a client that can access files and services on a variety of servers, called ____________________.
2. ____________________ is the name sometimes used to describe an organization that has a TLD (top-level domain) of com.
3. An Internet server called the ____________________ translates a domain name into its associated IP address, so data can route to the correct computer.
4. ____________________ is the phrase some people use to refer to the activity of jumping from one Web page to another.
5. On the Web, a(n) ____________________ is an organized set of topics, such as art, reference, sports, and subtopics.
6. A(n) ____________________ is a type of Web page that offers a variety of Internet services from a single, convenient location.
7. A(n) ____________________ is text that animates by scrolling across the screen.

8. One form of consumer-to-consumer e-commerce is a(n) ____________________, in which you bid on an item being sold by someone else.
9. HTML codes, called ____________________ specify how the text and other elements display in a browser and where the links lead.
10. Many FTP sites allow ____________________, whereby anyone can transfer some, if not all, available files.

Complete the Table

TOP-LEVEL DOMAIN (TLD) ABBREVIATIONS

TLD Abbreviations	Type of Domain
______	Commercial organizations, businesses, and companies
edu	______________________________
______	Government institutions
mil	______________________________
______	Network provider
org	______________________________
______	Business
pro	______________________________

Things to Think About

1. How is an ISP similar to, and different from, an online service? Which would you use to access the Internet? Why?
2. Compared to conventional commerce, what are the advantages, and disadvantages, of e-commerce? For what products is e-commerce most, and least, suited? Why?
3. Why is a moderated newsgroup considered more valuable than a newsgroup that is not moderated? What topics might be dealt with more effectively in a newsgroup that is not moderated? Why?
4. What netiquette rules or guidelines do you think are most important? What rules are least important? Why?

Puzzle

Write the word described by each clue in the puzzle below. Words can be written forward or backward, across, up and down, or diagonally. The initial letter of each word already appears in the puzzle.

M									A	B	
W					U				D		N
	M		D							N	
							L				
	A									C	
					B						
S	U								T		
				P							
		I								N	
					M	G		H	I		
S								O	M		

Appearance of motion created by displaying a series of still images

Music, speech, or any other sound

Communications lines that carry the heaviest traffic on the Internet

Software program that allows you to access and view Web pages

Computer that can access the contents of the storage area on a server

System on the Internet that stores domain names and their IP addresses

Provides high-speed connections over regular copper telephone lines

Financial business transaction that occurs over an electronic network

Digital representation of information such as a drawing or photograph

Starting page for a browser, similar to a book cover

Business that provides temporary Internet connections for a fee

Type of numerical address that uniquely identifies each Internet computer

Built-in connection to another related Web page or part of a Web page

Special software that displays Web pages on handheld computers

Reviews the contents of a newsgroup article and posts it, if appropriate

Defines a popular video compression standard

Code of acceptable behaviors users should follow while on the Internet

Online area in which users conduct written discussions about a subject

Program used to participate in a newsgroup

Supplies Internet access along with many members-only features

Telephone number dialed to connect to an access point on the Internet

Allows an e-commerce customer to collect purchases

Program that reads pages on Web sites in order to create a catalog of hits

Consists of an original newsgroup article and all subsequent replies

Copy a file from your computer to a Web site

Unique Web page address that tells a browser where to locate the page

Server automatically downloads content to your computer at regular intervals

Self Test Answers

Matching

1. *b* [p. 2.09]
2. *k* [p. 2.14]
3. *i* [p. 2.20]
4. *d* [p. 2.28]
5. *f* [p. 2.28]
6. *g* [p. 2.30]
7. *a* [p. 2.33]
8. *c* [p. 2.33]
9. *l* [p. 2.36]
10. *j* [p. 2.36]

True/False

1. *T* [p. 2.03]
2. *F* [p. 2.05]
3. *F* [p. 2.08]
4. *T* [p. 2.12]
5. *T* [p. 2.17]
6. *F* [p. 2.19]
7. *F* [p. 2.26]
8. *T* [p. 2.31]
9. *F* [p. 2.33]
10. *T* [p. 2.34]

Multiple Choice

1. *d* [p. 2.04]
2. *a* [p. 2.13]
3. *b* [p. 2.19]
4. *c* [p. 2.19]
5. *a* [p. 2.22]
6. *a* [p. 2.25]
7. *d* [p. 2.29]
8. *b* [p. 2.32]
9. *d* [p. 2.33]
10. *c* [p. 2.37]

Fill in the Blanks

1. *host computers* [p. 2.07]
2. *Dot com* [p. 2.08]
3. *DNS server* [p. 2.08]
4. *Surfing the Web* [p. 2.12]
5. *directory* [p. 2.15]
6. *portal Web page* or *portal* [p. 2.16]
7. *marquee* [p. 2.19]
8. *online auction* [p. 2.25]
9. *tags* [p. 2.28]
10. *anonymous FTP* [p. 2.33]

Complete the Table

TOP-LEVEL DOMAIN (TLD) ABBREVIATIONS

TLD Abbreviations	Type of Domain
com	Commercial organizations, businesses, and companies
edu	*Educational institutions*
gov	Government institutions
mil	*Military organizations*
net	Network provider
org	*Non-profit organizations*
biz	Business
pro	*Credentialed professional such as doctor or lawyer*

Things to Think About

Answers will vary.

Puzzle Answer

M	S	P	E	N	O	B	K	C	**A**	**B**	T
W	I	N	U	I	**U**	D	N	N	**D**	R	**N**
E	**M**	C	**D**	O	A	R	I	S	A	**N**	E
B	E	U	R	O	R	M	**L**	C	E	C	T
C	**A**	G	L	O	A	G	G	W	R	**C**	I
A	I	P	A	T	**B**	N	S	E	H	L	Q
S	**U**	H	I	P	I	R	M	W	**T**	I	U
T	P	O	P	**P**	E	M	O	G	E	E	E
I	N	**I**	P	A	O	M	E	W	P	**N**	T
N	P	O	D	C	R	P	O	D	S	T	T
G	H	E	E	E	**M**	**G**	S	**H**	**I**	E	E
S	R	O	T	A	R	E	D	**O**	**M**	A	R

DISCOVERING COMPUTERS 2003

STUDY GUIDE

CHAPTER 3

Application Software

Chapter Overview

This chapter begins by discussing the role of the system software with respect to application software. It then presents an overview of several productivity/business software applications, graphic design/multimedia software applications, home/personal/educational software applications, and communications software applications. The chapter identifies various Web applications. Finally, learning aids and support tools within application software products are presented.

Chapter Objectives

After completing this chapter, you should be able to:

- Define application software
- Understand how system software interacts with application software
- Identify the role of the user interface
- Explain how to start a software application
- Identify the widely used products and explain key features of productivity/business software applications, graphic design/multimedia software applications, home/personal/educational software applications, and communications software applications
- Identify various products available as Web applications
- Describe the learning aids available with many software applications

Chapter Outline

I. Application software [p. 3.02]

Application software consists ____

____

A software package is ____

A. The role of the system software [p. 3.03]

System software consists ____

____

The operating system contains ______________________________

____

The operating system must be loaded from the hard disk into the computer's memory before any application software can be run.

A utility program is ______________________________

____

B. The role of the user interface [p. 3.04]

The user interface controls ______________________________

____

A graphical user interface (GUI) combines ______________________________

____

C. Starting a software application [p. 3.04]

Both the Apple Macintosh and the Microsoft Windows operating systems use the concept of a desktop.

- The desktop is ______________________________

  ____

- An icon is ______________________________

  ____

- A button is ______________________________

  ____

- The pointer is ______________________________

  To click an object, you move ______________________________

  ____

- A menu contains ______________________________

  A command is ______________________________

  ____

  A submenu is ______________________________

You can start an application by clicking its name on a menu or submenu. Once started, an application displays in a window on the desktop.

- A window is ______________________________

  ____

  A title bar is ______________________________

- A dialog box is ______________________________

  ____

- A shortcut menu is ______________________________

  ____

II. Productivity/business software [p. 3.07]

Productivity software is ______________________________

____

A. Word processing software [p. 3.08]

Word processing software allows ______________________________

____

Word processing software features:

- Clip art is ______________________________
- Margins are ______________________________
- Wordwrap allows ______________________________
- Scrolling is ______________________________
- Find allows ______________________________

  Replace allows ______________________________
- A spelling checker reviews ______________________________

  ____
- A header is ______________________________

  A footer is ______________________________

B. Developing a document [p. 3.10]

Many applications, such as word processing, allow you to create, edit, format, save, and print documents.

- Creating involves ______________________________

  ____
- Editing is ______________________________

  ____
- Formatting involves ______________________________

  ____

  A font is ______________________________

  Font size specifies ______________________________

  Font style adds ______________________________
- Saving is ______________________________

  ____

  A file is ______________________________

  A file name is ______________________________
- Printing is ______________________________

  ____

1. Voice recognition [p. 3.11]
   Voice recognition is ____

   ____

C. Spreadsheet software [p. 3.12]
   With spreadsheet software, you can ____

   ____

   A worksheet is ____

1. Spreadsheet organization [p. 3.12]
   A spreadsheet file contains up to 255 related worksheets. On a worksheet, data is organized vertically in columns and horizontally in rows. A letter identifies each column, and a number identifies each row.
   A cell is ____
   Cells are identified by the column and row in which they are located (e.g., the cell at column B and row 10 is referred to as cell ________).
   Cells may contain three types of data:
   - ________________ (text)
   - ________________ (numbers)
   - ________________ (calculations performed on data)
2. Calculations [p. 3.12]
   A formula performs ____

   ____

   A function is ____

   ____

3. Macros [p. 3.13]
   A macro is ____

   ____

4. Recalculation [p. 3.13]
   A powerful spreadsheet feature is that when data changes, the rest of the data in a worksheet is recalculated automatically.
   What-if analysis is ____

   ____

5. Charting [p. 3.14]
   Charting shows the relationship of data in graphical form.
   - Line charts show ____

     ____

- Column charts display ______________________________

  ____

- Pie charts have ______________________________

  ____

D. Database software [p. 3.15]

A database is ______________________________

____

Database software allows ______________________________

____

Most PC databases consist of tables organized in rows and columns.

- A record is ______________________________

  ____

- A field is ______________________________

  ____

1. Database organization [p. 3.16]

   The table structure describes the records and fields in a table, including the number of fields, the field names, the field sizes, and the data types.

   Field names are short, descriptive, unique names assigned to each field.

   Field size is ______________________________

   Data type specifies ______________________________

   Common data types:

   - ____________ • ____________ • ____________
   - ____________ • ____________ • ____________
   - ____________

2. Entering data [p. 3.17]

   Populating is ______________________________

   ____

   Validation is ______________________________

   ____

3. Manipulating data [p. 3.17]

   Once records are entered, database software can be used to manipulate the data to generate information.

   - You can sort ______________________________

     ____

   - You can run a query, which is ______________________________

     ____

E. Presentation graphics software [p. 3.18]

Presentation graphics software allows ______________________________

____

Presentations can be viewed as slides, sometimes called a slide show.

A clip gallery includes ______________________________

____

A presentation can be viewed or printed in several formats:

- An outline includes ______________________________
- Audience handouts include ______________________________
- A notes page shows ______________________________

F. Personal information managers [p. 3.20]

A personal information manager (PIM) is ______________________________

____

Included in most PIMs:

- An appointment calendar allows ______________________________

  ____

- An address book maintains ______________________________

  ____

- A notepad is used to record ______________________________

  ____

G. Software suite [p. 3.20]

A software suite is ______________________________

____

Software suites offer two major advantages: ______________________________

____

H. Project management software [p. 3.21]

Project management software allows ______________________________

____

I. Accounting software [p. 3.21]

Accounting software helps ______________________________

____

III. Graphics and multimedia software [p. 3.22]

Power users often use sophisticated software to work with graphics and multimedia.

A. Computer-aided design [p. 3.22]

Computer-aided design (CAD) software is ______________________________

____

B. Desktop publishing software (for the professional) [p. 3.23]

Desktop publishing (DTP) software enables ____________________________

____

DTP software is designed to support page layout, which is _______________

____

A color library is ____

C. Paint/image editing software (for the professional) [p. 3.24]

Paint software (illustration software) allows ___________________________

____

Image editing software provides _________________________________

____

D. Video and audio editing software [p. 3.24]

Video consists ____

Video editing software can be used ______________________________

____

Audio is ____

Audio editing software can be used ______________________________

____

E. Multimedia authoring software [p. 3.25]

Multimedia authoring software allows _____________________________

____

F. Web page authoring software [p. 3.25]

Web page authoring software helps ______________________________

____

IV. Software for home, personal, and educational use [p. 3.26]

Most of the software in this category is inexpensive, costing less than $100.

A. Integrated software [p. 3.26]

Integrated software is ______________________________________

____

B. Personal finance software [p. 3.27]

Personal finance software is _________________________________

____

With online banking, you transfer ______________________________

____

C. Legal software [p. 3.28]

Legal software assists ______________________________

____

D. Tax preparation software [p. 3.28]

Tax preparation software guides ______________________________

____

E. Desktop publishing (for personal use) [p. 3.28]

Personal DTP software can ______________________________

____

F. Paint/image editing software (for personal use) [p. 3.29]

Personal paint/image editing software provides ______________________________

____

Photo editing software, a type of image editing software, allows __________

____

G. Clip art/image gallery [p. 3.30]

A clip art/image gallery is ______________________________

H. Home design/landscaping software [p. 3.30]

Home design/landscaping software assists ______________________________

____

I. Educational/reference/entertainment software [p. 3.30]

- Educational software is ______________________________

  ____

  Computer-based training (CBT) is ______________________________

  ____

- Reference software provides ______________________________

  ____

- Personal computer entertainment software includes __________

  ____

V. Software for communications [p. 3.32]

Users have a variety of software options relative to communications.

A. Electronic mail software [p. 3.32]

E-mail (electronic mail) is ______________________________

____

E-mail software is used ______________________________

____

B. Web browsers [p. 3.32]

A Web browser, or browser, allows ______________________________

____

C. Chat rooms [p. 3.32]

A chat room permits ______________________________

____

A chat client is ______________________________

D. Newsgroups [p. 3.32]

A newsgroup is ______________________________

____

A newsreader is ______________________________

E. Instant messaging [p. 3.32]

Instant messaging (IM) is ______________________________

____

An instant messenger is ______________________________

____

F. Groupware [p. 3.33]

Groupware is ______________________________

____

G. Videoconferencing [p. 3.33]

A videoconference is ______________________________

____

____

VI. Applications on the Web [p. 3.33]

A Web application is ______________________________

____

A. Web-based training [p. 3.34]

Web-based training (WBT) is ______________________________

____

Distance learning (DL) is ______________________________

____

B. Application service providers [p. 3.35]

An application service provider (ASP) is ______________________________

____

There are five categories of ASPs:

- ____
- ____
- ____
- ____
- ____

VII. Learning aids and support tools within an application [p. 3.36]

Learning aids provided by many applications and Web sites:

- Online Help is ____

  ____

  Often, Help is context-sensitive, meaning ____________________________

  ____

- An FAQ (Frequently Asked Questions) page helps ______________________

  ____

- A wizard is ____

  ____

Self Test

Matching

1. ____ computer-aided design (CAD) software
2. ____ desktop publishing (DTP) software
3. ____ paint software
4. ____ multimedia authoring software
5. ____ personal finance software
6. ____ legal software
7. ____ tax preparation software
8. ____ home design/landscaping software
9. ____ educational software
10. ____ e-mail software

a. used to prepare legal documents and provide legal advice to individuals
b. used to combine text, graphics, audio, video, and animation into an interactive presentation
c. used to create, send, receive, forward, store, print, and delete electronic mail messages
d. used in creating engineering, architectural, and scientific designs
e. used to balance a checkbook, pay bills, track income and expenses, and track investments
f. used to guide individuals or small businesses through the process of filing federal taxes
g. used to draw pictures, shapes, and other graphical images with various on-screen tools
h. used to edit digital photographs by removing red-eye or adding special effects
i. used to create Web pages, in addition to organizing and maintaining Web sites
j. used to design and produce sophisticated documents containing text and graphics
k. used to assist with the design or remodeling of a house, deck, or yard
l. used to teach a particular skill, from a foreign language to how to cook

True/False

____ 1. A graphical user interface (GUI) requires the typing of keywords or pressing of special keys on the keyboard to enter data and instructions.

____ 2. Shortcut menus display a list of commands commonly used to complete a task related to the current activity or selected item.

____ 3. A header is text that appears at the bottom of each page.

____ 4. Formatting is important because the overall look of a document can affect its ability to communicate effectively.

____ 5. Only a small fraction of the columns and rows in a spreadsheet displays on the computer screen at one time.

____ 6. In a database, a field contains information about a given person, product, or event, while a record contains a specific piece of information within a field.

____ 7. Presentation graphics software provides an array of predefined presentation formats that define complementary colors and other items on the slides.

____ 8. Most PIMs do not include an appointment calendar, address book, or notepad.

____ 9. Unlike a software suite, the applications within an integrated software package use different interfaces and have entirely unique features.

____ 10. To access a Web application, you simply visit the Web site that offers the program.

Multiple Choice

____ 1. What is loaded, or copied, into memory from the computer's hard disk each time you start your computer?
   a. the operating system
   b. a software application
   c. the software package
   d. a utility program

____ 2. What is a title bar?
   a. a small image that displays on the screen to represent a program
   b. an onscreen work area that uses common graphical elements
   c. a horizontal space at the top of a window that contains the window's name
   d. an instruction that causes a computer program to perform a specific action

____ 3. What happens when you format a document?
   a. text, numbers, or graphical images are inserted using an input device
   b. changes are made to the document's existing content
   c. the appearance of the document is changed
   d. the document is copied from memory to a storage medium

____ 4. How many rows and columns does a spreadsheet typically have?
   a. 256 columns and 256 rows
   b. 65,536 columns and 65,536 rows
   c. 65,536 columns and 256 rows
   d. 256 columns and 65,536 rows

____ 5. What common data type includes Web addresses that link a document to a Web page?
   a. numeric
   b. hyperlink
   c. memo
   d. currency

____ 6. In a personal information manager (PIM), for what purpose is a notepad used?
   a. to record ideas, reminders, and other important information
   b. to schedule activities for a particular day and time
   c. to enter and maintain names, addresses, and telephone numbers
   d. to design and produce sophisticated documents

____ 7. What type of software might a general contractor use to manage a home-remodeling schedule or a publisher use to coordinate the process of producing a textbook?
   a. home design/landscaping software
   b. project management software
   c. desktop publishing software
   d. presentation graphics software

____ 8. What type of software can be used to modify sound clips and usually includes filters designed to enhance sound quality?
   a. audio editing software
   b. video editing software
   c. image editing software
   d. photo editing software

____ 9. What type of software products often use a computer-based training (CBT) approach?
   a. educational software
   b. home design/landscaping software
   c. reference software
   d. clip art/image gallery software

____ 10. What does word processing software use to help you create memorandums, meeting agendas, fax cover sheets, and letters?
   a. online help
   b. FAQs
   c. tutorials
   d. wizards

Fill in the Blanks

1. A(n) ____________________ is a specific software product, such as Microsoft Word.
2. A(n) ____________________ is a type of system software that performs a specific task, usually related to managing a computer, its devices, or its programs.
3. A(n) ____________________ is a program that copies itself into other programs and spreads through multiple computers.
4. A single ____________________ is about 1/72 of an inch in height.
5. ____________________ is the computer's capability of distinguishing spoken words.

6. The number of fields, field names, field sizes, and data types in a database table collectively are referred to as the table ____________________.
7. You can specify the data a query retrieves by identifying ____________________, which are restrictions the data must meet.
8. Some chat rooms support ____________________, where you hear and see others and they can hear or see you as you chat.
9. Home users today can make a(n) ____________________, where both parties see each other as they talk.
10. Microsoft's Web applications, called ____________________, enable users to access Microsoft software on the Web from any type of device or computer.

Complete the Table

POPULAR SOFTWARE PACKAGES FOR HOME/PERSONAL/EDUCATIONAL USE

Software Application	Popular Packages
____________________	• Microsoft Works
____________________	• Intuit Quicken • Microsoft Money
____________________	• Kiplinger's WILL Power • Quicken Lawyer
____________________	• Intuit TurboTax • Kiplinger TaxCut
____________________	• Corel GALLERY • Nova Development Art Explosion
____________________	• Broderbund 3D Home Design Suite • Quality Plans Complete LandDesigner
____________________	• Microsoft Encarta • Rand McNally TripMaker

Things to Think About

1. What word processing features would be most useful to an author composing a short story? To a publicist creating a newsletter? To a student writing a term paper? Why?
2. Why is a spreadsheet's capability to perform what-if analysis important to business executives?
3. What types of software would be particularly useful to business travelers? Why?
4. What types of communications software would be most used by a teenager? A college student? A business professional? Why?

Puzzle

Use the given clues to complete the crossword puzzle.

Application Software

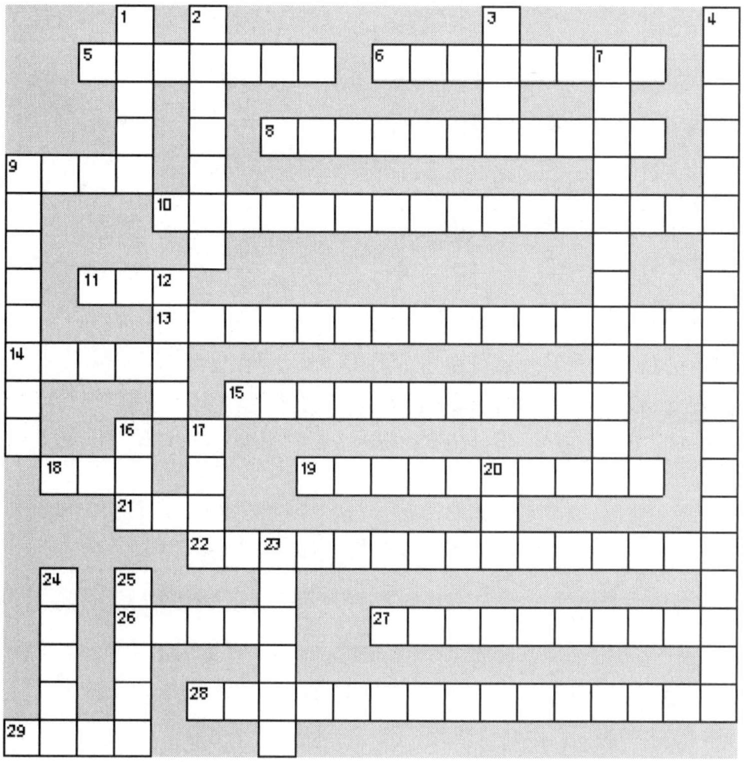

Across

5. PIM capability used to record ideas, reminders, and other information
6. Collection of data organized to allow access, retrieval, and use of the data
8. PIM capability in which names and addresses can be entered and maintained
9. Name assigned to a specific design of characters
10. Computer's capability of distinguishing spoken words
11. Interface that combines text, graphics, and other visual images
13. Type of Help information that relates to the current task
14. Any sound stored and produced by a computer
15. Transfer information between a handheld computer and a desktop computer
18. Type of education in which students learn by using computer exercises
19. DTP process of arranging text and graphics on a page-by-page basis
21. Software that helps organize personal information
22. A specific software product, such as Microsoft Word
26. Sequence of keystrokes and instructions that are recorded and saved
27. Software that combines applications into a single, easy-to-use package
28. Reviews the spelling of words in a document
29. Intersection of a spreadsheet column and row

Down

1. About 1/72 of an inch in height
2. On-screen work area that can display graphical elements
3. Type of page used to find answers to common questions
4. PIM capability used to schedule activities
7. Displays a list of commonly used commands for completing a task
9. Unique combination of characters that identifies a file
12. Small image that represents a program, document, or other object
16. Software used to produce sophisticated documents with text and graphics
17. Software used to create, access, and manage a database
20. Third-party organization that distributes software and services on the Web
23. Text that appears at the bottom of each page in a document
24. Collection of individual software applications sold as a single package
25. Transmission of messages via a computer network

Self Test Answers

Matching

1. *d* [p. 3.22]
2. *j* [p. 3.23]
3. *g* [p. 3.24]
4. *b* [p. 3.25]
5. *e* [p. 3.27]
6. *a* [p. 3.28]
7. *f* [p. 3.28]
8. *k* [p. 3.30]
9. *l* [p. 3.30]
10. *c* [p. 3.32]

True/False

1. *F* [p. 3.04]
2. *T* [p. 3.06]
3. *F* [p. 3.09]
4. *T* [p. 3.10]
5. *T* [p. 3.12]
6. *F* [p. 3.16]
7. *T* [p. 3.18]
8. *F* [p. 3.20]
9. *F* [p. 3.27]
10. *T* [p. 3.33]

Multiple Choice

1. *a* [p. 3.03]
2. *c* [p. 3.06]
3. *c* [p. 3.10]
4. *d* [p. 3.12]
5. *b* [p. 3.16]
6. *a* [p. 3.20]
7. *b* [p. 3.21]
8. *a* [p. 3.24]
9. *a* [p. 3.30]
10. *d* [p. 3.37]

Fill in the Blanks

1. *software package* [p. 3.02]
2. *utility program* or *utility* [p. 3.03]
3. *virus* [p. 3.03]
4. *point* [p. 3.10]
5. *Voice recognition* or *Speech recognition* [p. 3.11]
6. *structure* [p. 3.16]
7. *criteria* [p. 3.17]
8. *voice chats* or *video chats* [3.32]
9. *video telephone call* [p. 3.33]
10. *.NET* [p. 3.34]

Complete the Table

POPULAR SOFTWARE PACKAGES FOR HOME/PERSONAL/EDUCATIONAL USE

Software Application	Popular Packages
Integrated Software	• Microsoft Works
Personal Finance	• Intuit Quicken • Microsoft Money
Legal	• Kiplinger's WILL Power • Quicken Lawyer
Tax Preparation	• Intuit TurboTax • Kiplinger TaxCut
Clip Art/Image Gallery	• Corel GALLERY • Nova Development Art Explosion
Home Design/Landscaping	• Broderbund 3D Home Design Suite • Quality Plans Complete LandDesign

Software Application	Popular Packages
Reference	• Microsoft Encarta • Rand McNally TripMaker

Things to Think About

Answers will vary.

Puzzle Answer

Application Software

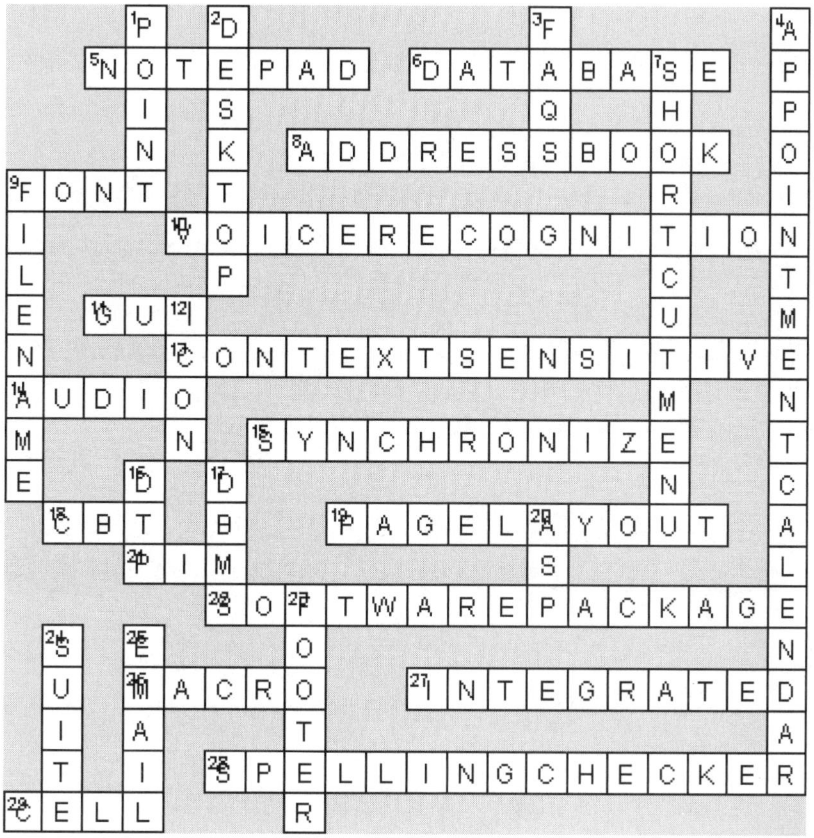

NOTES

DISCOVERING COMPUTERS 2003

STUDY GUIDE

CHAPTER 4

The Components of the System Unit

Chapter Overview

This chapter presents the components in the system unit. You learn how memory stores data, instructions, and information. The sequence of operations that occur when a computer executes an instruction is described. The chapter also includes a comparison of various personal computer processors on the market today.

Chapter Objectives

After completing this chapter, you should be able to:

- Describe the components in the system unit
- Explain how the CPU uses the four steps of a machine cycle to process data
- Compare and contrast various personal computer processors on the market today
- Define a bit and describe how a series of bits represents data
- Differentiate among the various types of memory
- Describe the types of expansion slots and cards in the system unit
- Explain the difference between a serial, a parallel, and a USB port
- Describe how buses contribute to a computer's processing speed
- Identify components in a notebook computer
- Identify components in a handheld computer

Chapter Outline

I. The system unit [p. 4.02]

The system unit is ____

____

- A desktop PC system unit usually is separate from the monitor and keyboard. Some system units sit on top of a desk. Other models, called tower models, stand ____
- An all-in-one computer houses ____

  ____

A. The motherboard [p. 4.04]

The motherboard is ______________________________

A chip is ______________________________

____

An integrated circuit is ______________________________

____

A transistor acts ______________________________

____

Types of chip packages:

- A dual inline package (DIP) consists ______________________________

  ____

- A pin grid array (PGA) package holds ______________________________

  ____

- A flip chip-PGA (FC-PGA) package is ______________________________

  ____

- A single edge contact (SEC) cartridge connects ______________________________

  ____

II. Central processing unit [p. 4.05]

The central processing unit (CPU or processor) interprets______________________________

____

Most devices connected to a computer communicate with the CPU to carry out a task. The CPU contains the control unit and the arithmetic/logic unit (ALU).

A. The control unit [p. 4.05]

The control unit directs______________________________

____

The control unit repeats a set of four basic operations called the machine cycle or instruction cycle:

- Fetching is______________________________
- Decoding is ______________________________
- Executing is ______________________________
- Storing is______________________________

Instruction time (i-time) is ______________________________

Execution time (e-time) is ______________________________

Some computer professionals measure a computer's speed in MIPS (**m**illions of **i**nstructions **p**er **s**econd).

CPUs use either a CISC or RISC design.

- CISC (complex instruction set computing) supports ____________________
  ____
- RISC (reduced instruction set computing) reduces ____________________
  ____

B. The arithmetic/logic unit [p. 4.07]

The arithmetic/logic unit (ALU) performs ____________________
____

- Arithmetic operations include____________________
- Comparison operations involve ____________________
- Logical operations use ____________________

C. Pipelining [p. 4.07]

With pipelining, the CPU begins ____________________
____

D. Registers [p. 4.07]

Registers are ____________________
____

E. The system clock [p. 4.08]

The system clock synchronizes ____________________
____

Each tick of the system clock is a clock cycle. Many of today's CPUs are superscalar and can ____________________

Clock speed is ____________________

Manufacturers state clock speed in megahertz and gigahertz.

- Megahertz (MHz) equates ____________________
- Gigahertz (GHz) equates ____________________

F. Comparison of personal computer processors [p. 4.09]

On a personal computer, all functions of the processor usually are on a single chip that some call a microprocessor.

Intel is a leading manufacturer of personal computer processors. Intel makes the Pentium®, Celeron™, Xeon™, and Itanium™ processors.

Intel-compatible processors have ____________________
____

A Motorola processor has____________________
____

An integrated CPU combines ______________________________

____

When buying a computer, processor speed is an important consideration. Today's processors use MMX™ (multimedia extension) technology. Intel's processors include SSE instructions (streaming single-instruction, multiple-data instructions), and AMD's processors have 3DNow!™ or 3DNow!™ Professional technology.

- MMX™ technology is ______________________________
- SSE instructions and 3DNow!™ technology further improve ______________

  ____

G. Processor installation and upgrades [p. 4.11]

A processor upgrade can increase a computer's performance.

Forms of upgrades:

- A chip for chip upgrade replaces ______________________________

  ____

- A piggyback upgrade stacks ______________________________

  ____

- A daughterboard upgrade puts the new processor chip on a daughterboard. A daughterboard is ______________________________

  ____

A socket is______________________________

A zero-insertion force (ZIF) socket has ______________________________

____

H. Heat sinks and heat pipes [p. 4.12]

Newer processors generate a lot of heat.

A heat sink is ______________________________

____

A heat pipe cools ______________________________

I. Coprocessors [p. 4.13]

A coprocessor is ______________________________

____

J. Parallel processing [p 4.13]

Parallel processing speeds processing time by using ______________

____

III. Data representation [p. 4.13]

Human speech is analog because ______________________________

____

Most computers are digital because they recognize ______________________________

____

Computers use the binary system, which has only two digits to represent the electronic states of off (0) and on (1).

A bit is______________________________

A byte is ______________________________

Patterns called coding schemes are used to represent data:

- ASCII is ______________________________
- EBCDIC is ______________________________
- Unicode is ______________________________

IV. Memory [p. 4.15]

Memory is______________________________

Memory stores:

(1) ______________________________

(2) ______________________________

(3) ______________________________

The stored program concept is ______________________________

____

An address is______________________________

Manufacturers state memory and storage sizes in terms of the number of bytes the device has available for storage.

- A kilobyte (KB or K) is ______________________________
- A megabyte (MB) is ______________________________
- A gigabyte (GB) is ______________________________

Memory can be volatile or nonvolatile.

Volatile memory loses ______________________________

Nonvolatile memory does______________________________

A. RAM [p. 4.17]

RAM (random access memory) consists ______________________________

____

Most RAM is volatile, so items needed in the future must be saved.

Saving is ______________________________

Basic types of RAM:

- Dynamic RAM (DRAM) chips must be ______________________________

  ____

  Variations of DRAM chips:

  Synchronous DRAM (SDRAM) chips are ______________________________

  ____

  Double data rate SDRAM (DDR SDRAM) chips are ______________________________

  ____

  Direct Rambus® DRAM (Direct RDRAM) chips are ______________________________

  ____

- Static RAM (SRAM) chips are ______________________________

  ____

1. RAM requirements [p. 4.18]

   The amount of RAM a computer requires depends ______________________________

   ____

B. Cache [p. 4.19]

Most of today's computers improve processing time with cache.

Memory cache stores ______________________________

Layers of memory cache:

- Level 1 (L1) cache is ______________________________
- Level 2 (L2) cache is ______________________________

  Advanced transfer cache is ______________________________
- L3 cache is ______________________________

C. ROM [p. 4.20]

ROM (read-only memory) refers ______________________________

____

- Firmware are ROM chips that contain ______________________________

  ____

- A PROM (programmable read-only memory) chip is ______________________________

  ____

- An EEPROM (electrically erasable programmable read-only memory) chip is ______________________________

D. Flash memory [p. 4.21]

Flash memory is ______________________________

____

Flash memory cards store ______________________________

E. CMOS [p 4.21]

CMOS (complementary metal-oxide semiconductor memory) stores ________

____

F. Memory access times [p. 4.22]

Access time is ____

____

Memory access times are measured in nanoseconds (billionths of a second).

V. Expansion slots and expansion cards [p. 4.23]

An expansion slot is ____

____

Types of expansion cards found in most of today's computers:

- ____________________
- ____________________
- ____________________
- ____________________

With Plug and Play, the computer can ____

____

A. PC Cards and flash memory cards [p. 4.24]

A PC Card is ____

____

Types of PC cards:

- Type I cards add ____
- Type II cards contain ____
- Type III cards house ____

Flash memory cards are used in many handheld computers and devices.

Hot plugging allows ____

VI. Ports [p. 4.25]

A port is ____

Ports have different types of connectors, which join a cable to a device.

- Male connectors have ____
- Female connectors have ____

A gender changer is ____

A. Serial ports [p. 4.27]

A serial port is ____

____

Serial ports connect ____

B. Parallel ports [p. 4.27]

A parallel port is ______________________________

____

Parallel ports connect ______________________________

C. Universal serial bus port [p. 4.28]

A USB port can ______________________________

____

Daisy chain to attach ______________________________

A USB hub plugs ______________________________

D. Special-purpose ports [p. 4.28]

1. 1394 port [p. 4.28]

   A 1394 port can ______________________________

2. MIDI port [p. 4.28]

   A MIDI (musical instrument digital interface) port connects ___________

   ____

3. SCSI port [p. 4.29]

   A SCSI (small computer system interface) port is ______________

   ____

4. IrDA port [p. 4.29]

   An IrDA (Infrared Data Association) port transmits ______________

   ____

VII. Buses [p. 4.29]

A bus is an electrical channel that allows ______________________________

____

The bus width, or size of the bus, determines ______________________________

Word size is ______________________________

Basic types of buses:

- A system bus is ______________________________
- An expansion bus allows ______________________________

A. Expansion bus [p. 4.30]

The types of expansion buses on the motherboard determine the types of expansion cards you can add.

Types of expansion buses:

- The ISA bus is ______________________________
- A local bus is ______________________________

- The AGP is ______________________________
- The USB eliminates ______________________________
- The PC Card bus is ______________________________

VIII. Bays [p. 4.32]

A bay is ______________________________

Drive bays most often hold ______________________________

- An external drive bay is ______________________________
- An internal drive bay is ______________________________

IX. Power supply [p. 4.32]

The power supply is ______________________________

____

An AC adapter is ______________________________

X. Mobile computers [p. 4.33]

Notebook computers and handheld computers have ______________________________

____

Self Test

Matching

1. ____ MIDI port
2. ____ ISA bus
3. ____ SCSI port
4. ____ VESA bus
5. ____ AGP
6. ____ PCI bus
7. ____ USB port
8. ____ 1394 bus
9. ____ IrDA port
10. ____ PC Card bus

a. bus that speeds processing by storing frequently used instructions and data

b. expansion bus for a PC Card that adds capabilities to a laptop computer

c. port used by wireless devices to transmit signals to a computer

d. port that can connect up to 127 different devices with a single connector

e. the most common and slowest expansion bus; connects to a mouse and modem card

f. first standard local expansion bus, which was used primarily for video cards

g. port designed to absorb and ventilate heat produced by electrical components

h. special high-speed parallel port used to attach disk drives and printers

i. bus designed by Intel to improve the speed with which 3-D graphics and video transmit

j. bus that eliminates the need to install expansion cards into expansion slots

k. special type of serial port designed to connect the system unit to a musical instrument

l. current local bus standard, used with video cards and high-speed network cards

True/False

____ 1. On a personal computer, the electronic components and most storage devices reside outside the system unit.

____ 2. The time it takes the control unit to fetch and decode an instruction is called instruction time or i-time, while the time it takes to execute and store an instruction is called execution time or e-time.

____ 3. A brand of Intel processor called the Xeon™ is designed for less expensive PCs.

____ 4. The American Standard Code for Information Interchange (ASCII) is used primarily on mainframe computers.

____ 5. When the computer is powered on, certain operating system files load from a storage device and remain in RAM as long as the computer is running.

____ 6. With a single inline memory module (SIMM), the pins on opposite sides of the circuit board do not connect and thus form two sets of contacts.

____ 7. Accessing data in memory can be more than 200,000 times slower than accessing data on a hard disk.

____ 8. An internal modem is a communications device that enables computers to communicate via telephone lines.

____ 9. Unlike other cards, a PC Card or flash memory card can be changed without having to open the system unit or restart the computer.

____ 10. An AC adapter converts a standard wall outlet's DC power of 5 to 12 volts to the AC power ranging from 115 to 120 volts that is required for use with a computer.

Multiple Choice

____ 1. On a personal computer, what normally is located *outside* the system unit?
   a. the keyboard and monitor
   b. the processor and memory module
   c. the ports and connectors
   d. all of the above

____ 2. In the machine cycle, what is the process of decoding?
   a. obtaining an instruction or data item from memory
   b. translating an instruction into a command a computer understands
   c. carrying out the commands
   d. writing a result to memory

____ 3. What processor, developed by Digital Equipment Corporation, is used primarily in workstations and high-end servers?
   a. the Celeron™ microprocessor
   b. the Motorola microprocessor
   c. the Pentium® microprocessor
   d. the Alpha microprocessor

____ 4. A group of eight bits, called a byte, provides enough different combinations of 0s and 1s to represent how many individual characters?
   a. 8
   b. 32
   c. 256
   d. 1024

____ 5. Which of the following is an example of volatile memory?
   a. RAM
   b. ROM
   c. CMOS
   d. flash memory

____ 6. Generally, home users running Windows and using standard application software such as word processing should have at least how much RAM?
   a. 8 MB
   b. 16 MB
   c. 32 MB
   d. 128 MB

____ 7. When a processor needs an instruction or data, in what order does it search memory?
   a. first RAM, then L1 cache, then L2 cache, then L3 cache (if it exists)
   b. first L3 cache (if it exists), then L1 cache, then RAM, then L2 cache
   c. first L2 cache, then L3 cache (if it exists), then RAM, then L1 cache
   d. first L1 cache, then L2 cache, then L3 cache (if it exists), then RAM

____ 8. What type of PC Cards house devices such as hard disks?
   a. Type I cards
   b. Type II cards
   c. Type III cards
   d. Type IV cards

____ 9. Originally developed as an alternative to the slower speed serial ports, parallel ports often are used to connect what to the system unit?
   a. a mouse
   b. a keyboard
   c. a modem
   d. a printer

____ 10. Like the clock speed at which a processor executes, the clock speed for a bus is measured in what unit?
   a. milliseconds (ms)
   b. megahertz (MHz)
   c. nanoseconds (ns)
   d. kilobytes (KB)

Fill in the Blanks

1. A(n) ________________ is one system clock cycle per second.
2. Users running engineering or graphics applications will notice a dramatic increase in speed in applications that take advantage of a(n) ________________.
3. Current processors include ________________, a type of L2 cache built directly on the processor chip.
4. ROM contains ________________, which is the sequence of instructions the computer follows to load the operating system and other files when it is turned on.
5. ROM chips called ________________ contain permanently written data, instructions, or information.
6. Programmers use ________________ instructions to program a PROM (programmable read-only memory) chip.

7. ________________ store flash memory on a removable disk instead of a chip.
8. PC Cards originally were called ________________ because they conform to standards developed by the Personal Computer Memory Card International Association.
9. A(n) ________________ plugs into a USB port on the system unit and contains multiple USB ports into which cables from USB devices are plugged.
10. A high-speed IrDA port, sometimes called a(n) ________________ port, is used with devices such as the keyboard, printer, digital cameras, and digital telephones.

Complete the Table

MEMORY AND STORAGE SIZES

Term	***Abbreviation***	***Approximate Memory Size***	***Approximate Number of Pages of Text***
______________	KB or K	1 thousand bytes	______________
Megabyte	______________	______________	500
______________	GB	______________	500,000
______________	______________	1 trillion bytes	500,000,000

Things to Think About

1. If you were to purchase a personal computer today, what type of processor would it have? Why?
2. Why do people upgrade their processors instead of buying a new computer? What form of processor upgrade seems easiest? Why?
3. How do coding schemes make it possible for humans to interact with computers? Why do people usually not realize that coding scheme conversions are occurring?
4. How is the system unit for a notebook computer similar to, and different from, the system unit for a desktop computer? Why do you think a notebook computer usually is more expensive than a desktop computer with the same capabilities?

Puzzle

Write the word described by each clue in the puzzle below. Words can be written forward or backward, across, up and down, or diagonally. The initial letter of each word already appears in the puzzle.

	S		S		C		U			M	C
					C		S				C
		H							A		
M									W		
P		R	A							R	
	B			M			C	P			
			P		A						
		B				R					
M				K					I		
		I		B							
	D		U			C					
S											

Box-like case that houses the electronic components of a computer

Main circuit board in the system unit

Microscopic pathway, etched on a chip, capable of carrying electrical current

Interprets and carries out the basic instructions that operate a computer

CPU component that directs and coordinates most computer operations

Unit in which some computer professionals measure a CPU's speed

CPU design that supports a large number of instructions

CPU design that reduces the instructions to only those used more frequently

CPU component that performs arithmetic, comparison, and logical operations

One system clock cycle per second

Opening in the motherboard into which a processor chip is inserted

Special additional chip or circuit board that assists the processor in performing certain tasks

Smallest unit of data a computer can represent

The most widely used coding system to represent data

Coding scheme capable of representing all the world's current languages

Temporary storage place for data, instructions, and information

Abbreviation for approximately 1,000 bytes

Abbreviation for approximately one million bytes

Abbreviation for approximately one billion bytes

Memory chips that can be read from and written to

Small circuit board on which RAM chips usually reside

Improves processing time in most of today's computers

Memory chips storing data that only can be read

Type of memory chip that stores configurations information about a computer

Thin, credit card-sized device that adds capabilities to a mobile computer

Interface, or point of attachment, of an external device to the system unit

Type of interface that connects devices by transmitting data one bit at a time

Type of interface that connects devices by transferring more than one bit at a time

Type of port that connects a musical instrument to the system unit

Type of high-speed, specialized parallel port

Type of port necessary for wireless devices to transmit signals to a computer

Channel that allows devices inside and attached to the system unit to communicate

Number of bits a processor can interpret and execute at a given time

Bus designed to improve the speed with which 3-D graphics and video transmit

Type of bus that eliminates the need to install cards into expansion slots

Open area inside the system unit into which additional equipment can be installed

Open space that most often holds disk drives

Self Test Answers

Matching

1. *k* [p. 4.28]
2. *e* [p. 4.31]
3. *h* [p. 4.29]
4. *f* [p. 4.31]
5. *i* [p. 4.31]
6. *l* [p. 4.31]
7. *d* [p. 4.28]
8. *j* [p. 4.32]
9. *c* [p. 4.29]
10. *b* [p. 4.32]

True/False

1. *F* [p. 4.02]
2. *T* [p. 4.06]
3. *F* [p. 4.10]
4. *F* [p. 4.14]
5. *T* [p. 4.16]
6. *F* [p. 4.18]
7. *F* [p. 4.22]
8. *T* [p. 4.23]
9. *T* [p. 4.25]
10. *F* [p. 4.32]

Multiple Choice

1. *a* [p. 4.03]
2. *b* [p. 4.05]
3. *d* [p. 4.10]
4. *c* [p. 4.14]
5. *a* [p. 4.18]
6. *c* [p. 4.19]
7. *d* [p. 4.20]
8. *c* [p. 4.24]
9. *d* [p. 4.27]
10. *b* [p. 4.30]

Fill in the Blanks

1. hertz [p. 4.08]
2. floating-point coprocessor [p. 4.13]
3. advanced transfer cache [p. 4.20]
4. basic input/output system (BIOS) [p. 4.20]
5. firmware [p. 4.20]
6. microcode [p. 4.20]
7. flash BIOS [p. 4.21]
8. PCMCIA cards [p. 4.24]
9. USB hub [p. 4.28]
10. FIR (fast infrared) port [p. 4.29]

Complete the Table

MEMORY AND STORAGE SIZES

Term	*Abbreviation*	*Approximate Memory Size*	*Approximate Number of Pages of Text*
Kilobyte	KB or K	1 thousand bytes	*1/2*
Megabyte	*MB*	*1 million bytes*	500
Gigabyte	GB	*1 billion bytes*	500,000
Terabyte	*TB*	1 trillion bytes	500,000,000

Things to Think About

Answers will vary.

Puzzle Answer

I	**S**	*C*	**S**	*I*	**C**	*R*	**U**	*S*	*O*	**M**	**C**
D		*T*	*E*	*K*	**C**	*O*	**S**	*L*	*O*	*E*	**C**
I	*S*	**H**	*R*	*S*	*P*	*S*	*B*	*T*	**A**	*M*	*O*
M	*Y*	*E*	*I*	*G*	*U*	*S*	*H*	*G*	**W**	*O*	*N*
P	*A*	**R**	**A**	*L*	*L*	*E*	*L*	*P*	*O*	**R**	*T*
S	**B**	*T*	*L*	**M**	*R*	*C*	**C**	**P**	*R*	*Y*	*R*
P	*E*	*Z*	**P**	*B*	**A**	*O*	*A*	*C*	*D*	*M*	*O*
I	*V*	**B**	*O*	*D*	*S*	**R**	*C*	*C*	*S*	*O*	*L*
M	*I*	*A*	*R*	**K**	*C*	*P*	*H*	*A*	**I**	*D*	*U*
T	*R*	**I**	*T*	**B**	*I*	*O*	*E*	*R*	*Z*	*U*	*N*
D	**D**		**U**	*N*	*I*	**C**	*O*	*D*	*E*	*L*	*I*
S	*Y*	*S*	*T*	*E*	*M*	*U*	*N*	*I*	*T*	*E*	*T*

NOTES

DISCOVERING COMPUTERS 2003

STUDY GUIDE

CHAPTER 5

Input

Chapter Overview

This chapter introduces input, the types of input, and input devices. The keyboard is characterized and different keyboard types are identified. Various pointing devices are introduced. You find out how a mouse works and discover different mouse types. Voice recognition is explained, and inputting data into a handheld computer is described. You learn the uses of digital cameras, the techniques used for video input, and the uses of PC video cameras and Web cams. Scanners and other reading devices are presented. Finally, input devices for physically challenged users are explored.

Chapter Objectives

After completing this chapter, you should be able to:

- Describe the two types of input
- List the characteristics of a keyboard
- Identify various types of keyboards
- Identify various types of pointing devices
- Explain how a mouse works
- Describe different mouse types
- Explain how voice recognition works
- Understand how to input data into a handheld computer
- Identify the uses of a digital camera
- Describe the various techniques used for video input
- Describe the uses of PC video cameras and Web cams
- Explain how scanners and other reading devices work
- Identify alternative input devices for physically challenged users

Chapter Outline

I. What is input? [p. 5.02]

Input is ____

____

Types of input:

- Data is ____

  ____

Information is ______________________________

____

- Instructions can ______________________________

  ____

  - A program is ______________________________

    ____

  - A command is ______________________________

    ____

    Most programs are menu-driven and have a graphical user interface.
    A menu-driven program provides ______________________________

    ____

    A graphical user interface (GUI) has ______________________________

    ____

  - A user response is ______________________________

    ____

II. What are input devices? [p. 5.04]
An input device is ______________________________

____

III. The keyboard [p. 5.04]
A keyboard is ______________________________

____

All computer keyboards have a typing area that includes letters of the alphabet, numbers, spaces, punctuation marks, and other basic keys. Many keyboards also have:

- A numeric keypad is ______________________________

  ____

- Function keys are ______________________________

  ____

- Arrow keys move ______________________________

  ____

  The insertion point is ______________________________
- Toggle keys are ______________________________

  ____

A. Keyboard types [p. 5.05]
- A QWERTY keyboard is ______________________________

  ____
- An enhanced keyboard has ______________________________

  ____
- A cordless keyboard is ______________________________

  ____
- A portable keyboard is ______________________________

  ____
- An ergonomic keyboard has ______________________________

  ____

  The goal of ergonomics is ______________________________

  ____

IV. Pointing devices [p. 5.07]

A pointing device is ______________________________

____

A pointer is ______________________________

V. Mouse [p. 5.07]

A mouse is ______________________________

____

A. Mouse types [p. 5.07]
- A mechanical mouse has ______________________________

  ____

  A mouse pad is ______________________________
- An optical mouse uses ______________________________

  ____
- A cordless mouse, or wireless mouse, is ______________________________

  ____

B. Using a mouse [p. 5.08]

As you move the mouse across a flat surface, the pointer on the screen also moves. When the pointer rests on an object, generally you press, or click, one of the mouse buttons to perform a certain action on that object.

VI. Other pointing devices [p. 5.10]

Although the mouse is the most widely used, some users work with other pointing devices.

A. Trackball [p. 5.10]
A trackball is ____

____

B. Touchpad [p. 5.10]
A touchpad, or trackpad, is ____

____

C. Pointing stick [p. 5.11]
A pointing stick is ____

____

D. Joystick and wheel [p. 5.11]
A joystick is ____

____

A wheel is ____

____

E. Light pen [p. 5.12]
A light pen is ____

____

F. Touch screen [p. 5.12]
A touch screen is ____

____

G. Stylus [p. 5.12]
A stylus looks ____

____

Architects, mapmakers, artists, and designers use a stylus or a cursor on a graphics tablet.
A graphics tablet is ____

____

A cursor is ____

____

Many handheld computers use handwriting recognition software that translates ____

VII. Voice input [p. 5.14]
Voice input is ____

____

Voice recognition is ____

____

- With speaker-dependent software, the computer makes ______________

  ____

- Speaker-independent software has ______________________

  ____

- Discrete speech requires ______________________

  ____

- Continuous speech allows ______________________

  ____

A. Audio input [p. 5.16]

   Audio input is ______________________

   ____

   Windows stores audio files as waveforms, which are called WAV files and have a .wav extension.

VIII. Input devices for handheld computers [p. 5.16]

Handheld computers are popular for home and business use. Data can be input into a handheld computer in many ways:

____

____

____

IX. Digital cameras [p. 5.18]

A digital camera allows ______________________

____

To work with images from a digital camera, you download (transfer a copy of) the images to a personal computer.

Basic types of digital cameras:

- A studio camera is ______________________

  ____

- A field camera is ______________________

  ____

- A point-and-shoot camera is ______________________

  ____

The quality of a digital camera is affected by its resolution.

Resolution describes ______________________

The higher the resolution, the better the image quality.

Some manufacturers use dots per inch to represent a digital camera's resolution.

A pixel is ______________________________

Dots per inch (dpi) is ______________________________

- Optical resolution is ______________________________
- Enhanced resolution uses ______________________________

X. Video input [p. 5.21]

Video input is ______________________________

____

To input video, the analog video signal must be converted into a digital signal.

A video capture card is ______________________________

____

A digital video (DV) camera is ______________________________

____

A. PC video cameras [p. 5.21]

A PC video camera is ______________________________

____

During a video telephone call, parties can see each other as they talk.

PC cameras and digital watermarks can connect printed media to the Web.

A digital watermark is ______________________________

____

B. Video compression [p. 5.22]

Like audio files, video files can require huge amounts of storage space. To decrease the size of the files, video often is compressed.

Video compression works ______________________________

____

A video decoder is ______________________________

A video digitizer can capture ______________________________

____

C. Web cams [p. 5.23]

A Web cam is ______________________________

____

A streaming cam shows ______________________________

____

D. Videoconferencing [p. 5.24]

A videoconference is ______________________________

____

A whiteboard is ______________________________

XI. Scanners and reading devices [p. 5.24]

A source document is ______________________________

Scanners and reading devices make the input process more efficient by capturing data directly from source documents.

A. Optical scanner [p. 5.25]

An optical scanner, or scanner, is ______________________________

____

- A flatbed scanner works ______________________________

  ____

Like a digital camera, the quality of a scanner is measured by its resolution. Businesses often use scanners for image processing.

Image processing consists ______________________________

____

An image processing system is ______________________________

____

OCR software can ______________________________

B. Optical readers [p. 5.27]

An optical reader is ______________________________

____

Types of optical readers:

1. Optical character recognition [p. 5.27]

   Optical character recognition (OCR) is ______________________________

   ____

   Most OCR devices include ______________________________

   ____

   OCR characters often are used on turnaround documents. A turnaround document is ______________________________

2. Optical mark recognition [p. 5.28]

   Optical mark recognition (OMR) devices read ______________________________

   ____

3. Bar code scanner [p. 5.28]

   A bar code scanner uses ______________________________

   A bar code is ______________________________

   ____

C. Magnetic-ink character recognition reader [p. 5.30]

   A magnetic-ink character recognition (MICR) reader can ______________________________

   ____

   The banking industry almost exclusively uses MICR for check processing.

D. Wireless input [p. 5.30]

   Wireless input technology can be used to obtain data directly at the location where a transaction or event takes place. This technology often is used where the environment is difficult to control. Devices with wireless connections to the Web can be used to send data to central office computers.

XII. Input devices for physically challenged users [p. 5.31]

The Americans with Disabilities Act (ADA) requires ______________________________

____

A keyguard is ______________________________

____

Other options for users with limited hand mobility are keyboards with larger keys and screen-displayed keyboards.

A head-mounted pointer is ______________________________

____

With gesture recognition, the computer will ______________________________

____

Self Test

Matching

1. ____ QWERTY keyboard
2. ____ enhanced keyboard
3. ____ cordless keyboard
4. ____ portable keyboard
5. ____ mouse
6. ____ trackball
7. ____ touchpad
8. ____ pointing stick
9. ____ joystick
10. ____ light pen

a. handheld input device that contains a light source or can detect light

b. light-sensing input device that reads printed text and graphics and then transmits the results

c. keyboard with 12 function keys, 2 CTRL keys, 2 ALT keys, and arrow keys

d. provides multiple users with an area on which they can write or draw

e. vertical lever mounted on a base, moved to control the actions of a vehicle or player

f. pressure-sensitive pointing device shaped like a pencil eraser, positioned between keys

g. full-sized keyboard that can be attached to and removed from handheld computers

h. standard computer keyboard named because of the layout of its typing area

i. small, flat, rectangular pointing device that is sensitive to pressure and motion

j. widely used pointing device designed to fit comfortably under the palm of your hand

k. stationary pointing device with a ball on its top that is rotated with the thumb or fingers

l. battery-powered device that transmits data using a technology such as radio waves

True/False

____ 1. A graphical user interface is the least user-friendly way to interact with a computer.

____ 2. The command associated with a function key depends on the program you are using.

____ 3. An optical mouse is less precise than a mechanical mouse, but it also is slightly less expensive.

____ 4. A pointing stick does not need additional desk space and does not require cleaning like a mechanical mouse or trackball.

____ 5. WAV files usually are small — requiring less than 1 MB of storage space for several minutes of audio.

____ 6. All handheld computers use the same handwriting recognition software.

____ 7. The smaller the number of pixels a digital camera uses to capture an image, the better the quality of the image.

____ 8. A video decoder is less effective and efficient than video compression software.

____ 9. To participate in a videoconference, you need videoconferencing software, a microphone, speakers, and a video camera mounted on your computer.

____ 10. The banking industry almost exclusively uses MICR (magnetic-ink character recognition) for check processing.

Multiple Choice

____ 1. The timecards for a given week are an example of what type of input?

a. programs
b. user responses
c. commands
d. data

____ 2. In many programs, what function key can be pressed to display a Help window?

a. F1
b. F2
c. F3
d. F4

____ 3. What key is a toggle key that can be used to switch between two different states?

a. PAGE UP
b. NUM LOCK
c. PRINT SCREEN
d. BACKSPACE

____ 4. What is the most widely used pointing device on desktop computers?

a. the touchpad
b. the trackball
c. the joystick
d. the mouse

____ 5. What pointing device is found more often on notebook computers?

a. the mouse
b. the touchpad
c. the joystick
d. the trackball

____ 6. What input device often is used in kiosks located in stores, hotels, airports, and museums?
a. joysticks
b. touch screens
c. pointing sticks
d. touchpads

____ 7. A 1,600 x 1,200 dpi digital camera has how many pixels?
a. 1,600 down the vertical edge and 1,200 across the horizontal edge
b. 1,600 per vertical inch and 1,200 per horizontal inch
c. 1,600 across the horizontal edge and 1,200 down the vertical edge
d. 1,600 per horizontal inch and 1,200 per vertical inch

____ 8. What device captures data directly from source documents?
a. optical scanners
b. ergonomic keyboards
c. pointing devices
d. all of the above

____ 9. What type of bar code is used by the national mail service?
a. POSTNET — Postal Numeric Encoding Technique
b. Codabar
c. UPC — Universal Product Code
d. Code 39

____ 10. What do you use to press the keys on a screen-displayed keyboard?
a. a digital camera
b. a scanner
c. a pointing device
d. a whiteboard

Fill in the Blanks

1. The ____________________, is a symbol that indicates where on the screen the next character you type will display.
2. The goal of ____________________ is to incorporate comfort, efficiency, and safety into the design of items in the workplace.
3. A(n) ____________________ is a rectangular rubber or foam pad that provides better traction for a mouse than the top of a desk.
4. Some graphics tablets use a(n) ____________________, which is a device that looks similar to a mouse, except that it has a window with cross hairs.
5. Special software along with a pen and graphics tablet allow businesses to save time using ____________________, which are just as legal as an ink signature.
6. Windows stores audio files as ____________________.
7. To work with the images from a digital camera, you ____________________, or transfer a copy of, the pictures to a desktop personal computer.

8. Because it records video as digital signals, with a(n) ____________________ you do not need a video capture card.
9. ____________________ allows you to convert paper documents such as reports, memos, and procedure manuals into an electronic form.
10. Computers with a capability called ____________________ have the potential to recognize sign language, read lips, track facial movements, or follow eye gazes.

Complete the Table

MOUSE OPERATIONS

Operation	Mouse Action
__________________	Move the mouse across a flat surface until the pointer is positioned on the item of choice on the desktop.
__________________	Press and release the primary mouse button, which usually is the left mouse button.
__________________	Press and release the secondary mouse button, which usually is the right mouse button.
__________________	Quickly press and release the primary mouse button twice without moving the mouse.
__________________	Point to an item, hold down the left mouse button, move the item, and then release the left mouse button.
__________________	Point to an item, hold down the right mouse button, move the item, and then release the right mouse button.
__________________	Roll the wheel forward or backward.
__________________	Press the wheel button while moving the mouse on the desktop.

Things to Think About

1. Two types of input are data and instructions (programs, commands, and user responses). What type of input device (keyboard, pointing devices, scanners, and so on) can be used to enter each type of input?
2. How is a notebook computer keyboard different from a desktop computer keyboard? What keys might be left off of, or serve more than one purpose on, a notebook keyboard?

3. What pointing device would you most like to have with a desktop computer? What pointing device would you most like to have with a notebook computer? Why?
4. How do scanners and reading devices make the input process more efficient and accurate? For what, if any, types of input are scanners and reading devices unsuitable? Why?

Puzzle

The terms described by the phrases below are written below each line in code. Break the code by writing the correct term above the coded word. Then, use your code to translate the final sentence.

1. Any data or instructions entered into the memory of a computer	______ RMKFG
2. Collection of facts, figures, and symbols that is processed into information	______ WZGZ
3. Type of program that provides lists as a means of entering commands	______ NVMF-WIREVM
4. Commonly used input device containing keys that are pressed to enter data	______ PVBYLZIW
5. Calculator-style arrangement of keys on a computer keyboard	______ MFNVIRX PVBKZW
6. Symbol that indicates where on the screen the next character typed will appear	______ RMHVIGRLM KLRMG
7. Four keys: one pointing up, one pointing down, one pointing left, and one pointing right	______ ZIILD PVBH
8. Key that switches between two different states, often indicated by status lights	______ GLTTOV PVB
9. Small symbol on the screen that usually takes the shape of a block arrow, I-beam, or pointing hand	______ KLRMGVI
10. Input device often used with game software and flight simulation software	______ QLBHGRXP
11. Allows you to tap areas of the display with your finger to enter data	______ GLFXS HXIVVM
12. How Windows stores audio files; the files have a .wav extension	______ DZEVULINH
13. Allows you to take and store photographed images digitally instead of on traditional film	______ WRTRGZO XZNVIZ
14. Factor that describes the sharpness and clearness of an image	______ IVHLOFGRLM
15. Can be used to capture and save an individual frame from an analog video	______ ERWVL WRTRGRAVI
16. Meeting between geographically separated people who use a network or the Internet to transmit data	______ ERWVLXLMUVIVMXV

17. Original form of data captured with scanners or reading devices ______ HLFIXV WLXFNVMG
18. Light-sensing input device that reads printed material and translates it into a form the computer can use ______ HXZMMVI
19. Type of document designed to be returned to the company that creates and sends it ______ GFIMZILFMW
20. Identification consisting of a set of vertical lines and spaces of different widths ______ YZI XLWVH

______

GBKRHGH FHRMT GSV NLOGILM PVBYLZIW, DSRXS RH HKORG ZMW

______

XLMGLFIVW GL URG VZXS SZMW DRGS GSV NLHG XLNNLMOB FHVW PVBH

______

FMWVI GSV HGILMTVHG URMTVIH, XZM GBKV NLIV GSZM GSIVV GRNVH

______

UZHGVI GSZM GBKRHGH FHRMT Z GIZWRGRLMZO PVBYLZIW.

Self Test Answers

Matching

1. *h* [p. 5.05]
2. *c* [p. 5.05]
3. *l* [p. 5.05]
4. *g* [p. 5.06]
5. *j* [p. 5.07]
6. *k* [p. 5.10]
7. *i* [p. 5.10]
8. *f* [p. 5.11]
9. *e* [p. 5.11]
10. *a* [p. 5.12]

True/False

1. *F* [p. 5.03]
2. *T* [p. 5.04]
3. *F* [p. 5.07]
4. *T* [p. 5.11]
5. *F* [p. 5.16]
6. *F* [p. 5.17]
7. *F* [p. 5.20]
8. *F* [p. 5.21]
9. *T* [p. 5.24]
10. *T* [p. 5.30]

Multiple Choice

1. *d* [p. 5.03]
2. *a* [p. 5.04]
3. *b* [p. 5.04]
4. *d* [p. 5.07]
5. *b* [p. 5.10]
6. *b* [p. 5.12]
7. *b* [p. 5.20]
8. *a* [p. 5.24]
9. *a* [p. 5.29]
10. *c* [p. 5.32]

Fill in the Blanks

1. *insertion point* [p. 5.04]
2. *ergonomics* [p. 5.06]
3. *mouse pad* [p. 5.07]
4. *cursor* [p. 5.13]
5. *electronic signatures* or *e-signatures* [p. 5.13]
6. *waveforms* or *WAV files* [p. 5.16]
7. *download* [p. 5.18]
8. *digital video camera* or *DV camera* [p. 5.21]
9. *Image processing* or *Imaging* [p. 5.26]
10. *gesture recognition* [p. 5.32]

Complete the Table

MOUSE OPERATIONS

Operation	Mouse Action
Point	Move the mouse across a flat surface until the pointer is positioned on the item of choice on the desktop.
Click	Press and release the primary mouse button, which usually is the left mouse button.
Right-click	Press and release the secondary mouse button, which usually is the right mouse button.
Double-click	Quickly press and release the primary mouse button twice without moving the mouse.

Operation	Mouse Action
Drag	Point to an item, hold down the left mouse button, move the item, and then release the left mouse button.
Right-drag	Point to an item, hold down the right mouse button, move the item, and then release the right mouse button.
Rotate wheel	Roll the wheel forward or backward.
Press wheel button	Press the wheel button while moving the mouse on the desktop.

Things to Think About

Answers will vary.

Puzzle Answer

1. Any data or instructions entered into the memory of a computer — *input* — RMKFG
2. Collection of facts, figures, and symbols that is processed into information — *data* — WZGZ
3. Type of program that provides lists as a means of entering commands — *menu-driven* — NVMF-WIREVM
4. Commonly used input device containing keys that are pressed to enter data — *keyboard* — PVBYLZIW
5. Calculator-style arrangement of keys on a computer keyboard — *numeric keypad* — MFNVIRX PVBKZW
6. Symbol that indicates where on the screen the next character typed will appear — *insertion point* — RMHVIGRLM KLRMG
7. Four keys: one pointing up, one pointing down, one pointing left, and one pointing right — *arrow keys* — ZIILD PVBH
8. Key that switches between two different states, often indicated by status lights — *toggle key* — GLTTOV PVB
9. Small symbol on the screen that usually takes the shape of a block arrow, I-beam, or pointing hand — *pointer* — KLRMGVI
10. Input device often used with game software and flight simulation software — *joystick* — QLBHGRXP

11.	Allows you to tap areas of the display with your finger to enter data	*touch screen* GLFXS HXIVVM
12.	How Windows stores audio files; the files have a .wav extension	*waveforms* DZEVULINH
13.	Allows you to take and store photographed images digitally instead of on traditional film	*digital camera* WRTRGZO XZNVIZ
14.	Factor that describes the sharpness and clearness of an image	*resolution* IVHLOFGRLM
15.	Can be used to capture and save an individual frame from an analog video	*video digitizer* ERWVL WRTRGRAVI
16.	Meeting between geographically separated people who use a network or the Internet to transmit data	*videoconference* ERWVLXLMUVIVMXV
17.	Original form of data captured with scanners or reading devices	*source document* HLFIXV WLXFNVMG
18.	Light-sensing input device that reads printed material and translates it into a form the computer can use	*scanner* HXZMMVI
19.	Type of document designed to be returned to the company that creates and sends it	*turnaround* GFIMZILFMW
20.	Identification consisting of a set of vertical lines and spaces of different widths	*bar code* YZI XLWVH

Typists using the Moltron keyboard, which is split and
GBKRHGH FHRMT GSV NLOGILM PVBYLZIW, DSRXS RH HKORG ZMW

contoured to fit each hand with the most commonly used keys
XLMGLFIVW GL URG VZXS SZMW DRGS GSV NLHG XLNNLMOB FHVW PVBH

under the strongest fingers, can type more than three times
FMWVI GSV HGILMTVHG URMTVIH, XZM GBKV NLIV GSZM GSIVV GRNVH

faster than typists using a traditional keyboard.
UZHGVI GSZM GBKRHGH FHRMT Z GIZWRGRLMZO PVBYLZIW.

DISCOVERING COMPUTERS 2003

STUDY GUIDE

CHAPTER 6

Output

Chapter Overview

Data is a collection of raw, unprocessed facts, figures, and symbols. Computers process and organize data into information, which has meaning and is useful. Computers then output this information to users. This chapter describes the various methods of output and several commonly used output devices. Output devices presented include display devices, printers, speakers, data projectors, fax machines, multifunction devices, and terminals.

Chapter Objectives

After completing this chapter, you should be able to:

- Define the four categories of output
- Identify the different types of display devices
- Describe factors that affect the quality of a display device
- Identify monitor ergonomic issues
- Explain the differences among various types of printers
- Describe the uses of speakers and headsets
- Identify the purpose of data projectors, fax machines, and multifunction devices
- Explain how a terminal is both an input and output device
- Identify output options for physically challenged users

Chapter Outline

I. What is output? [p. 6.02]

Output is ____

____

Common types of output:

- Text consists ____

  ____

- Graphics are ____

  ____

- Audio is ____
  ____
- Video consists ____
  ____

II. What are output devices? [p. 6.04]

An output device is ____

____

III. Display devices [p. 6.04]

A display device is ____

____

The information displayed, or soft copy, exists ____

____

A display device consists of a screen, or projection surface, and the components that produce the information on the screen.

A monitor is ____

Most display devices are color, but some are monochrome and use gray scaling.

- Monochrome means ____
- Gray scaling involves ____

Display devices include CRT monitors, LCD monitors and displays, gas plasma monitors, and televisions.

A. CRT monitors [p. 6.05]

A CRT monitor is ____

____

A cathode ray tube (CRT) is ____

____

The dots of phosphor material that coat a CRT screen combine to form pixels.

A pixel is ____

A monitor's viewable size is ____

____

B. LCD monitors and displays [p. 6.05]

LCD monitors and LCD displays use ____

____

A liquid crystal display (LCD) has ____

____

LCD monitors and LCD displays are types of flat-panel displays.

A flat-panel display has ____

____

LCD monitors and displays produce color using either active matrix or passive-matrix technology.

- An active-matrix, or thin-film transistor (TFT), display uses __________

  ____

  Organic TFT uses ____
- A passive-matrix display uses ____

  ____

  High-performance addressing (HPA) provides ____________________

  ____

C. Gas plasma monitors [p. 6.08]

A gas plasma monitor is ____

____

D. Quality of display devices [p. 6.08]

CRT monitor quality depends largely on its resolution, dot pitch, and refresh rate. LCD monitor quality depends primarily on resolution.

1. CRT quality [p. 6.08]
   - Resolution describes ____

     ____
   - Dot pitch is ____

     ____
   - Refresh rate is ____

     ____
2. LCD quality [p. 6.09]

   The resolution of an LCD monitor or display generally is __________

   ____

E. Video cards and monitors [p. 6.10]

A video card converts ____

____

The number of colors a video card can display is determined by its bit depth.

Bit depth is ____

____

Both the video card and the monitor must support the same video standard to generate the desired resolution and number of colors. Most current video cards support the super video graphics array (SVGA) standard.

Video cards use video memory to store information about each pixel.

F. Monitor ergonomics [p. 6.11]

Many monitors have features to address ergonomic issues:________________

____

____

Electromagnetic radiation (EMR) is ________________________________

____

The ENERGY STAR program encourages __________________________

____

G. Televisions [p. 6.12]

Connecting a computer to a standard television requires an NTSC converter.

An NTSC converter converts ____________________________________

____

High-definition television (HDTV) is _____________________________

____

IV. Printers [p. 6.12]

A printer is ____

____

Printed information, or hard copy, exists ___________________________

____

- Portrait orientation is _____________________________________
- Landscape orientation is ___________________________________

With Internet printing, an Internet service on the Web sends ________________

____

Generally, printers are either impact or nonimpact.

A. Impact printers [p. 6.14]

An impact printer forms ______________________________________

____

Commonly used impact printers are dot-matrix printers and line printers.

1. Dot-matrix printers [p. 6.14]

A dot-matrix printer is _____________________________________

____

Dot-matrix printers use continuous-form paper, which connects ________

____

2. Line printers [p. 6.14]

A line printer is ______________________________

____

Popular types of line printers:

- A band printer prints ______________________________

____

- A shuttle-matrix printer moves ______________________________

____

B. Nonimpact printers [p. 6.15]

A nonimpact printer forms ______________________________

____

Commonly used nonimpact printers are ink-jet printers, laser printers, and thermal printers.

C. Ink-jet printers [p. 6.15]

An ink-jet printer is ______________________________

____

____

D. Laser printers [p. 6.16]

A laser printer is ______________________________

____

____

Laser printers use software to interpret a page description language (PDL).

A PDL tells ______________________________

Common PDLs:

- PCL is ______________________________
- PostScript is ______________________________

E. Thermal printers [p. 6.19]

A thermal printer generates ______________________________

____

Special types of thermal printers:

- A thermal wax-transfer printer generates ______________________________

____

- A dye-sublimation printer uses ______________________________

____

Some printers are used for special purposes, such as photo printers, label and postage printers, portable printers, and plotters and large-format printers.

F. Photo printers [p. 6.20]

A photo printer is ____

____

G. Label and postage printers [6.21]

A label printer is ____

____

H. Portable printers [p. 6.22]

A portable printer is ____

____

I. Plotters and large-format printers [p. 6.22]

Plotters are ____

____

A large-format printer creates ____

____

V. Speakers and headsets [p. 6.23]

An audio output device is ____

____

Commonly used audio output devices are speakers and headsets.

- Speakers are ____

  A woofer boosts ____
- With a headset, only you can ____

Voice output occurs ____

____

Internet telephony allows ____

____

VI. Other output devices [p. 6.24]

Many output devices are available for particular uses and applications:

A. Data projectors [p. 6.25]

A data projector is ____

____

- An LCD projector uses ____

  ____

- A digital light processing (DLP) projector uses ____________________

  ____

B. Facsimile (fax) machine [p. 6.25]

A facsimile (fax) machine is ____________________

____

A fax modem is ____________________

____

C. Multifunction devices [p. 6.26]

A multifunction device (MFD) is ____________________

____

VII. Terminals [p. 6.27]

A terminal is ____________________

____

- A dumb terminal has ____________________

  ____

  A host computer performs ____________________

  ____

- An intelligent terminal has ____________________

  ____

Special-purpose terminals:

- A point-of-sale (POS) terminal records ____________________

  ____

- An automatic teller machine (ATM) is ____________________

  ____

VIII. Output devices for physically challenged users [p. 6.29]

Output devices available for users with disabilities include ____________________

____

____

A Braille printer outputs ____________________

Self Test

Matching

1. ____ dot-matrix printer
2. ____ band printer
3. ____ shuttle-matrix printer
4. ____ ink-jet printer
5. ____ laser printer
6. ____ thermal printer
7. ____ photo printer
8. ____ label printer
9. ____ portable printer
10. ____ large-format printer

a. small, lightweight printer used with a notebook or handheld computer

b. uses a row of charged wires to draw an electrostatic pattern on specially coated paper

c. generates images by pushing electrically heated pins against heat-sensitive paper

d. produces images when tiny wire pins on a print head mechanism strike an inked ribbon

e. high-speed, high-quality nonimpact printer operating in a manner similar to a copy machine

f. prints fully-formed characters when hammers strike a horizontal, rotating band

g. used by graphic artists to create photo-realistic quality color prints

h. uses one or more colored pens or a scribing device to draw on paper or transparencies

i. produces photo lab quality pictures as well as printing everyday documents

j. forms characters and graphics by spraying tiny drops of liquid ink

k. prints on an adhesive-type material that can be placed on a variety of items

l. moves a series of print hammers back and forth horizontally at incredibly high speeds

True/False

____ 1. In the past, CRT monitor screens were flat, but current models have slightly curved screens to reduce eyestrain and fatigue.

____ 2. LCD monitors and displays are ideal for mobile users or users with space limitations.

____ 3. A monitor with higher resolution uses a smaller number of pixels, providing a rougher image.

____ 4. The number of colors that a video card can display is determined by its bit depth, or the number of bits it uses to store information about each pixel.

____ 5. Currently, all U.S. television stations broadcast digital signals, but by 2006, all stations must broadcast analog signals, as mandated by the FCC.

____ 6. Some companies use NLQ (near letter quality) impact printers for routine jobs such as printing mailing labels, envelopes, and invoices.

____ 7. With an ink-jet printer, a higher dpi means the drops of ink are larger, which provides a lower quality image.

____ 8. PostScript is used in fields such as desktop publishing and graphic art because it is designed for complex documents with intense graphics and colors.

____ 9. When using a headset, anyone within listening distance can hear the output.

____ 10. An advantage of an MFD is that it is significantly less expensive than if you purchase a printer, scanner, copy machine, and fax machine separately.

Multiple Choice

____ 1. What do many Web sites use to give images the appearance of motions?
   a. text
   b. animated graphics
   c. audio
   d. video

____ 2. How is monitor size measured?
   a. in square inches, stating the area of the screen
   b. vertically, from the top-left corner to the bottom-left corner
   c. horizontally, from the top-left corner to the top-right corner
   d. diagonally, from one corner of the casing to the other

____ 3. What do notebook and handheld computers often use?
   a. CRT monitors
   b. gas plasma monitors
   c. LCD displays
   d. all of the above

____ 4. On what does the quality of a monitor or display depend?
   a. its resolution
   b. its dot pitch
   c. its refresh rate
   d. all of the above

____ 5. Which of the following is *not* a commonly used type of impact printer?
   a. ink-jet printers
   b. dot-matrix printers
   c. band printers
   d. shuttle-matrix printers

____ 6. What type of nonimpact printer typically costs more than ink-jet printers, but also are much faster?
a. dot-matrix printers
b. thermal printers
c. line printers
d. laser printers

____ 7. What tells a laser printer how to layout the contents of a printed page?
a. a digital language processor (DLP)
b. a language character display (LCD)
c. a page description language (PDL)
d. a nonimpact language quantifier (NLQ)

____ 8. What type of printer often can read media directly from a digital camera, without the aid of a computer?
a. thermal printers
b. photo printers
c. portable printers
d. postage printers

____ 9. What type of smaller, lower-cost data projector uses tiny mirrors to reflect light, producing crisp, bright, colorful images that remain in focus and can be seen clearly even in a well-lit room?
a. an LCD projector
b. a large-format projector
c. a digital light processing (DLP) projector
d. an electrostatic projector

____ 10. What has no processing power and thus cannot function as an independent device?
a. a dumb terminal
b. an intelligent terminal
c. a programmable terminal
d. a host terminal

Fill in the Blanks

1. A(n) ____________________ is a small, book-sized computer that allows users to read, save, highlight, bookmark, and add notes to online text.

2. Refresh rate is measured according to ____________________, which is the number of times per second a screen is redrawn.

3. The Digital Display Working Group (DDWG) is developing a standard digital interface, called the ____________________, which provides connections for both CRT and LCD monitors.

4. The ____________________, which consists of video card and monitor manufacturers, develops video standards.

5. ____________________ is a set of standards that defines acceptable levels of EMR (electromagnetic radiation) for a monitor.
6. ____________________ is a two-way communications technology in which users interact with television programming.
7. A hard copy, also called a(n) ____________________, can be portrait or landscape orientation.
8. A laser printer creates images using powdered ink, called ____________________, and a laser beam.
9. A(n) ____________________ is digital postage you buy and print right from your personal computer.
10. Dumb terminals connect to a(n) ____________________ that performs the processing and then sends the output back to the dumb terminal.

Complete the Table

VIDEO STANDARDS

Standard	Suggested Resolution	Possible Simultaneous Colors
Monochrome Display Adapter (MDA)	____________	________________
______________________________	640 x 480	________________
	____________	256
Extended Graphics Array (XGA)	1024 x 768	________________
	____________	65,536
______________________________	800 x 600	________________
	1280 x 1024	________________
Beyond SVGA	____________	16.7 million
	2048 x 1536	________________

Things to Think About

1. Why is output printed on paper, which is a flexible material, called hard copy while output displayed on a screen, which is firm to the touch, is called soft copy?
2. Why are LCD monitors more expensive than CRT monitors? What advantages do LCD monitors offer over CRT monitors? Will LCD monitors ever replace CRT monitors? Why or why not?

3. Using Figure 6-15 (page 6.13), answer each question about your current printer requirements. Based on your answers, what type of printer would you be most likely to buy? Why?
4. How important is audio to you? Would you consider adding higher-quality stereo speakers, a woofer, or a headset to your personal computer? Why or why not?

Puzzle

All of the words described below appear in the puzzle. Words may be either forward or backward, across, up and down, or diagonal. Circle each word as you find it.

Output

```
                M
              R C D
            T E H B M
          O C T A M P Q
        W X F N R X P O J
            Q I A Q O
          A I R C U R E
        M L G P T R T E I
      T D P O P E A R L D G
          W U I R T A A
        S T D H D A I N D
      S R E S O L U T I O N
    H D C E O C T P A M M F U
        R P F H I P D R L
      F H A T R R H I E Z K
    E A E C C U E G P T L D P
  R H G R S O O M N M A C C I Z
      V T D P S E F O L R H
    A S Z N Y C D D W T E G S
  K O H L A T R O T I N O M Y H
F P I X E L J E M T C V H J I Z G
              E X K
              N A T
              U F G
```

Data that has been processed into a useful form

Characters used to create words, sentences, and paragraphs

Letter, number, or other symbol requiring one byte of storage space

Digital representation of nontext information

Music, speech, or any other sound

Images played back at speeds that provide the appearance of motion

Information shown on a display device

Display device consisting of a screen housed in a plastic or metal case

Front of a cathode ray tube

Single point in an electronic image

Type of display that does not use CRT

Sharpness or clarity of a monitor

Vertical distance between pixels on a monitor

Speed with which the monitor redraws images on the screen

Measure of refresh rate

Converts digital output into an analog signal

Standard supported today by just about every monitor

Output device that produces text and graphics on a physical medium

Orientation taller than it is wide

Orientation wider than it is tall

Unit in which dot-matrix printer speed is measured

Unit in which ink-jet printer resolution is measured

Unit in which ink-jet printer speed is measured

Tells a laser printer how to layout a page

Page description language commonly used in desktop publishing

Powdered ink used by laser printers

Communications device that transmits computer-prepared documents

Single piece of equipment that provides the functionality of a printer, scanner, and copy machine

Device that performs both input and output

Self-service banking machine

Self Test Answers

Matching

1. *d* [p. 6.14]
2. *f* [p. 6.15]
3. *l* [p. 6.15]
4. *j* [p. 6.15]
5. *e* [p. 6.16]
6. *c* [p. 6.19]
7. *i* [p. 6.20]
8. *k* [p. 6.21]
9. *a* [p. 6.22]
10. *g* [p. 6.22]

True/False

1. *F* [p. 6.05]
2. *T* [p. 6.05]
3. *F* [p. 6.09]
4. *T* [p. 6.10]
5. *F* [p. 6.12]
6. *T* [p. 6.14]
7. *F* [p. 6.15]
8. *T* [p. 6.18]
9. *F* [p. 6.23]
10. *T* [p. 6.27]

Multiple Choice

1. *b* [p. 6.03]
2. *d* [p. 6.05]
3. *c* [p. 6.06]
4. *d* [p. 6.08]
5. *a* [p. 6.14]
6. *d* [p. 6.17]
7. *c* [p. 6.18]
8. *b* [p. 6.20]
9. *c* [p. 6.25]
10. *a* [p. 6.27]

Fill in the Blanks

1. *electronic book (e-book)* [p. 6.07]
2. *hertz* [p. 6.09]
3. *Digital Video Interface (DVI)* [p. 6.10]
4. *Video Electronics Standards Association (VESA)* [p. 6.10]
5. *MPR II* [p. 6.11]
6. *Interactive TV* [p. 6.12]
7. *printout* [p. 6.12]
8. *toner* [p. 6.17]
9. *e-stamp* or *Internet stamp* [p. 6.21]
10. *host computer* [p. 6.27]

Complete the Table

VIDEO STANDARDS

Standard	Suggested Resolution	Possible Simultaneous Colors
Monochrome Display Adapter (MDA)	*720 x 350*	*1 for text*
Video Graphics Array (VGA)	640 x 480	*16*
	320 x 200	256
Extended Graphics Array (XGA)	1024 x 768	*256*
	640 x 480	65,536
Super Video Graphics Array (SVGA)	800 x 600	*16.7 million*
Beyond SVGA	*1920 x 1440*	16.7 million
	2048 x 1536	*16.7 million*

Things to Think About

Answers will vary.

Puzzle Answer

Output

DISCOVERING COMPUTERS 2003

STUDY GUIDE

CHAPTER 7

Storage

Chapter Overview

Storage refers to the media on which data, instructions, and information are kept. This chapter explains various storage media and storage devices. Storage media covered include floppy disks, high-capacity disks, hard disks, CD-ROMs, CD-RWs, DVD-ROMs, DVD+RWs, tape, and PC Cards and other miniature forms of storage. Enterprise storage systems also are covered.

Chapter Objectives

After completing this chapter, you should be able to:

- Differentiate between storage and memory
- Identify various types of storage media and storage devices
- Explain how a floppy disk stores data
- Identify the advantages of using high-capacity disks
- Describe how a hard disk organizes data
- Identify the advantages of using an Internet hard drive
- Explain how a compact disc stores data
- Understand how to care for a compact disc
- Differentiate among CD-ROMs, CD-RWs, DVD-ROMs, and DVD+RWs
- Identify the uses of tape
- Understand how an enterprise storage system works
- Explain how to use PC Cards and other miniature storage media
- Identify uses of microfilm and microfiche

CHAPTER OUTLINE

I. Storage [p. 7.02]

A. Memory [p. 7.03]

Memory, which is composed of one or more chips on the motherboard or some other circuit board in the computer, is a temporary holding place for data and instructions.

Types of memory:

- Volatile memory loses ______________________________

  ____
- Nonvolatile memory does not lose ______________________________

  ____

B. Storage [p. 7.04]

Storage holds ______________________________

____

A storage medium is ______________________________

____

A storage device is ______________________________

____

Storage devices function as sources of both input and output.

- Reading is ______________________________

  ____
- Writing is ______________________________

  ____

Access time is ______________________________

Capacity is ______________________________

II. Floppy disks [p. 7.06]

A floppy disk is ______________________________

____

Today, the standard floppy disk is ______________________________

A. Floppy disk drives [p. 7.06]

A floppy disk drive (FDD) is ______________________________

____

When you insert a floppy disk into a floppy disk drive, the drive slides the shutter (a metal cover over an opening in the disk's plastic shell) to the side to expose a portion of the recording surface. The read/write head in the drive reads items from or writes items on the floppy disk.

To read from or write on a floppy disk, the floppy disk drive must support the floppy disk's density.

Density is ______________________________

A disk with a higher density has a larger storage capacity. Most disks today are high density (HD). An HD floppy disk has ______________________________

Floppy disks are downward compatible, which means ____________________

____

Floppy disks are not upward compatible, and thus cannot ____________________

____

B. How a floppy disk stores data [p. 7.08]

Magnetic media uses ____

____

Floppy disks store data in tracks and sectors.

- A track is ____
- A sector is ____
- A cluster is ____

Formatting is ____

C. Care of floppy disks [p. 7.09]

When handling a floppy disk, avoid ________________________________

____

____

A write-protect notch is ____

____

If the write-protect notch is closed, the drive can write on the floppy disk.

III. High-capacity disks [p. 7.09]

A high-capacity disk drive is ____

____

A high-capacity disk often is used to back up important data and information.

A backup is ____

Types of high-capacity disk drives:

- A SuperDisk™ drive reads ____

  ____

- The HiFD™ (High Capacity FD) reads ________________________________

  ____

- A Zip® drive is ____

  ____

IV. Hard disks [p. 7.10]

Hard disks provide far larger storage capacities and much faster access times than floppy disks.

A hard disk consists ____

____

A platter is ____

An optically-assisted hard drive combines ______________________________

____

A. How a hard disk works [p. 7.11]

Most hard disks have multiple platters, stacked on top of one another. Each platter has a read/write head for each side.

A cylinder is ____

____

The platters spin continually at a high rate of speed, with the read/write heads floating on a cushion of air just above the platter surface.

A head crash occurs ____

Access time for hard disks is faster than for floppy disks because:

(1) ____

(2) ____

Disk cache is ____

A cache controller manages ____

A formatted hard disk can be divided into partitions. Each partition functions as if it were ____

B. Hard disk controllers [p. 7.13]

A disk controller is ____

____

A hard disk controller (HDC) is ____

Many external hard drives use a USB port as their interface.

Types of HDC controllers for personal computers:

1. EIDE [p. 7.13]

   Enhanced Integrated Drive Electronics (EIDE) controllers can __________

   ____

2. SCSI [p. 7.13]

   Small computer system interface (SCSI) controllers can ______________

   ____

C. Removable hard disks [p. 7.13]

A removable hard disk is ____

____

The Peerless™ disk and the Jaz® disk are ______________________________

____

Advantages of portable media: ______________________________

____

D. RAID [p. 7.14]

RAID (redundant array of independent disks) is ______________________

____

RAID improves reliability through the duplication of data, instructions, and information. Duplication is implemented in different ways, depending on the storage design, or level, used.

- Mirroring (level 1) is ______________________________
- Striping is ______________________________

E. Maintaining data stored on a hard disk [p. 7.15]

To prevent loss of data, you should perform preventative maintenance such as

____

F. Internet hard drives [p. 7.16]

An Internet hard drive is ______________________________

____

Reasons people use Internet hard drives:

- ______________________________
- ______________________________
- ______________________________
- ______________________________
- ______________________________

V. Compact discs [p. 7.17]

A compact disc (CD) is ______________________________

____

CDs store items using microscopic pits (indentations) and land (flat areas) in a single, spiral track. A high-powered laser light creates the pits, and a lower-powered laser reads items by reflecting light through the disc. The reflected light is converted into a series of bits that the computer can process.

A jewel box is ______________________________

Guidelines for proper care of compact discs:

- Do not expose ______________________________
- Do not stack ______________________________

- Do not touch ______________________________
- Do not eat ______________________________
- Do store ______________________________
- Do hold ______________________________

VI. CD-ROMs [p. 7.20]

A CD-ROM is ______________________________

____

The contents of a standard CD-ROM are recorded by the manufacturer and cannot be erased or modified.

A CD-ROM drive is ______________________________

A CD-ROM can hold ______________________________

A. CD-ROM drive speed [p. 7.20]

The speed of a CD-ROM is ______________________________

____

CD-ROM drives use an X to denote the original data transfer rate of 150 KB per second. A 48X CD-ROM drive has a data transfer rate of 7200 (48 x 150) KB per second, or 7.2 MB per second. The higher the data transfer rate, the smoother the playback of images and sounds.

B. PhotoCDs and Picture CDs [p. 7.21]

- A PhotoCD is ______________________________

  ____

  A PhotoCD is multisession, which means ______________________________

  ____

  Most standard CD-ROMs are single-session because ______________________________

  ____

- A Picture CD is ______________________________

  ____

C. CD-Rs and CD-RWs [7.22]

- A CD-R is ______________________________

  ____

  A CD recorder is used to ______________________________

- CD-RW is ______________________________

  ____

  A CD-RW drive is used ______________________________

A multiread CD-ROM drive is ______________________________

VII. DVD-ROMs and DVD+RWs [p. 7.24]

A DVD-ROM (digital versatile disc-ROM) is ______________________________

____

A DVD-ROM drive can read ______________________________

DVD-ROMs increase storage capacity using one of three storage techniques:

____

____

____

A. DVD+RW and other DVD variations [p. 7.25]

You can obtain recordable and rewritable versions of DVD.

- A DVD-R allows ______________________________

  ____

- With a DVD+RW you can ______________________________

  ____

  DVD+RAM is a competing technology to DVD+RW.

VIII. Tape [p. 7.26]

Tape is ______________________________

____

- A tape drive reads ______________________________
- A tape cartridge is ______________________________
- A tape library is ______________________________

Tape requires sequential access, which refers ______________________________

____

Floppy disks, hard disks, and compact discs use direct access, which means _____

____

IX. Enterprise storage systems [p. 7.27]

An enterprise storage system is ______________________________

____

Techniques used in enterprise storage systems:

- A server stores data, information, and instructions need on the network.
- A RAID system ensures data is not lost if one drive fails.
- A tape library is a high-capacity tape system that works with multiple tape cartridges.
- A CD-ROM jukebox holds ______________________________

- Companies using Internet backup store ______________________________

  ____

- A network-attached storage (NAS) device is ______________________________

  ____

- A storage area network (SAN) is ______________________________

  ____

A data warehouse is ____

X. PC Cards [p. 7.28]

A PC Card is ____

____

The advantage of a PC Card is ______________________________

XI. Miniature mobile storage media [p. 7.28]

Various types of miniature storage media are available for handheld devices.

A. Smart cards [p. 7.29]

A smart card ____

____

Types of smart cards:

- An intelligent smart card contains ______________________________

  ____

- A memory card has ____

Smart cards are used ____

____

____

Electronic money is ____

____

XII. Microfilm and microfiche [p. 7.26]

Microfilm and microfiche store microscopic images of documents.

Microfilm uses ____

Microfiche uses ____

A computer output microfilm (COM) recorder is ______________________________

____

Self Test

Matching

1. ____ floppy disk
2. ____ hard disk
3. ____ RAID
4. ____ CD-ROM
5. ____ DVD-ROM
6. ____ tape
7. ____ PC Card
8. ____ smart card
9. ____ microfilm
10. ____ microfiche

a. extremely high-capacity compact disc capable of storing from 4.7 GB to 17 GB

b. uses a small sheet of film to store microscopic images of documents

c. portable, inexpensive, flexible storage medium enclosed in a square-shaped plastic shell

d. magnetically coated ribbon capable of storing large amounts of data at a low cost

e. similar in size to a credit card, stores data on a thin microprocessor embedded in the card

f. consists of several inflexible, circular platters that store items electronically

g. thin, credit-card sized device that fits into a slot on a notebook or other personal computer

h. sequential access storage medium whose contents are lost when power is turned off

i. a group of two or more integrated hard disks, usually more reliable than traditional disks

j. uses a 100- to 215-foot roll of film to store microscopic images of documents

k. temporarily holds data and instructions while they are being processed by the CPU

l. silver-colored compact disc that uses the same laser technology used for recording music

True/False

____ 1. Storage, also called secondary storage, auxiliary storage, or mass storage, holds items such as data, instructions, and information for future use.

____ 2. Even if a file consists of only a few bytes, it uses an entire cluster of a floppy disk for storage.

____ 3. On a floppy disk, if the write-protect notch is open, the drive can write on the floppy disk.

____ 4. A Zip® drive is downward compatible with floppy disks; that is, it can read from and write on standard floppy disks as well as Zip® disks.

____ 5. Current personal computer hard disks can store from 10 to 75 GB of data, instructions, and information.

____ 6. If a hard disk has only one partition, the operating system designates it as drive A.

____ 7. The RAID technique called striping offers data duplication, but does not improve disk access times.

____ 8. To use a compact disc, push a button to slide out a tray, insert the compact disc with the label side down, and then push the button to close the tray.

____ 9. CD-R drives read at speeds of up to 24X and write at speeds of up to 8X.

____ 10. The goal of an enterprise storage system is to consolidate storage so operations run as efficiently as possible.

Multiple Choice

____ 1. How much data can a typical floppy disk store?
   a. 1.44 KB (approximately 1.44 thousand bytes)
   b. 1.44 MB (approximately 1.44 million bytes)
   c. 1.44 GB (approximately 1.44 billion bytes)
   d. 1.44 TB (approximately 1.44 trillion bytes)

____ 2. If a computer has two floppy disk drives, what is the second drive designated?
   a. drive A
   b. drive B
   c. drive C
   d. drive D

____ 3. What is the smallest unit of disk space that stores data?
   a. a track
   b. a sector
   c. a cluster
   d. a cylinder

____ 4. How can you maximize a floppy disk's life?
   a. keep the disk in a storage tray when not in use
   b. place the disk near magnetic fields
   c. open the disk's shutter or touch the recording surface
   d. expose the disk to excessive heat, sunlight, or cold

____ 5. What contaminant on a hard disk surface could cause a head crash and make the hard disk drive unusable?
   a. a hair
   b. dust
   c. smoke
   d. all of the above

____ 6. What popular, reasonably priced, removable hard disk by Iomega can store up to two gigabytes (GB)?
a. SuperDisk™ disk
b. HiFD™ disk
c. Zip® disk
d. Jaz® disk

____ 7. What Windows utility frees up space on a hard disk by listing files that can be deleted safely?
a. Disk Defragmenter
b. Disk Cleanup
c. Compression Agent
d. Resource Meter

____ 8. What should you do to care properly for a compact disc?
a. hold the disc by its edges
b. stack discs
c. touch the underside of the disc
d. eat, smoke, or drink near the disc

____ 9. What speed CD-ROM would have a data transfer rate of 7200 KB or 7.2 MB per second?
a. 8X
b. 16X
c. 32X
d. 48X

____ 10. What do libraries use to store back issues of newspapers, magazines, and genealogy records?
a. floppy disks and hard disks
b. CD-ROMs and DVD-ROMs
c. PC Cards and smart cards
d. microfilm and microfiche

Fill in the Blanks

1. When a computer's power is turned off, ____________________ loses its contents.
2. ____________________ is the process of preparing a disk for reading and writing.
3. A(n) ____________________ is a duplicate of a file, program, or disk that can be used if the original is lost, damaged, or destroyed.
4. A(n) ____________________ is slightly larger than and about twice as thick as a 3.5-inch floppy disk, and can store 100 MB or 250 MB of data.
5. Sometimes called a(n) ____________________, the hard disk inside the system unit of most desktop portable computers is not portable.
6. A(n) ____________________ occurs when a read/write head touches the surface of a hard disk platter, usually resulting in a loss of data.

7. An earlier type of EIDE controller was ____________________, which is short for AT Attachment.
8. Originally called a(n) ____________________________, a CD-RW overcomes the major disadvantage of CD-R disks, which is that you can write on them only once.
9. You must have a DVD+RW drive or a(n) ____________________ to write on DVD+RW discs.
10. A(n) ____________________ is the device that records images onto microfilm or microfiche.

Complete the Table

CHARACTERISTICS OF A 3.5-INCH HIGH DENSITY FLOPPY DISK

Capacity	____________________
Number of sides	____________________
____________________________	80
Sectors per track	____________________
____________________________	512
Sectors per disk	____________________

Things to Think About

1. How is downward compatible different from upward compatible? Why are floppy disk drives downward compatible but not upward compatible?
2. How does partitioning make hard disks more efficient?
3. How is an EIDE controller different from a SCSI controller? When would each controller be used?
4. Will compact discs, such as CD-ROMs or DVD-ROMs, someday replace magnetic media, such tape or floppy disk, or other media such as microfilm, or microfiche? Why or why not?

Puzzle

Use the given clues to complete the crossword puzzle.

Storage

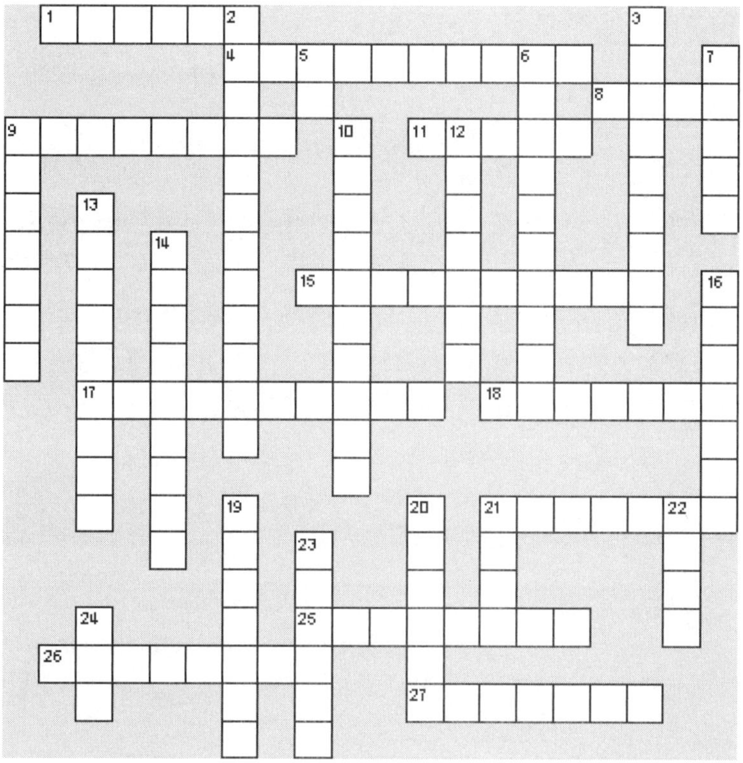

Across

1. Extremely high capacity compact disc
4. Minimum time it takes a storage device to locate an item on a disk
8. A group of two or more integrated hard disks
9. RAID storage design that splits items across multiple disks in the array
11. Narrow recording band that forms a full circle on a disk surface
15. Separate areas into which a hard disk can be divided, each of which functions as a separate hard disk drive
17. Portable, inexpensive storage medium
18. Small arcs into which a disk's tracks are broken
21. Metal covering an opening in a floppy disk's plastic shell
25. The size of a storage device
26. Usually consists of several inflexible, circular disks on which data is stored electronically
27. The number of bits in an area on a storage medium

Down

2. One of the first storage media used with mainframe computers
3. Occurs when a read/write head touches the surface of a hard disk platter
5. Flat, round, portable metal storage medium, usually 4.75 inches in diameter
6. Stores images of documents on sheet film
7. Silver-colored compact disc that can contain text, graphics, video, and sound
9. Holds items such as data, instructions, and information for future use
10. Process of preparing a disk for reading and writing by organizing the disk into storage locations
12. Process of transferring items from a storage medium into memory
13. Stores images of documents on roll film
14. Simplest RAID storage design with one backup disk for each disk
16. Consists of two to eight sectors
19. Process of transferring items from memory to a storage medium
20. Thin, credit card-sized device that fits into a personal computer expansion slot
21. Controller that can support multiple disk drives, as well as other peripherals
22. The most widely used controller, or interface, for hard disks
23. Duplicate of a file, program, or disk that can be used if the original is lost
24. High-speed network that connects storage devices

Self Test Answers

Matching

1. *c* [p. 7.06]
2. *f* [p. 7.10]
3. *i* [p. 7.14]
4. *l* [p. 7.20]
5. *a* [p. 7.25]
6. *d* [p. 7.26]
7. *g* [p. 7.28]
8. *e* [p. 7.29]
9. *j* [p. 7.30]
10. *b* [p. 7.30]

True/False

1. *T* [p. 7.04]
2. *T* [p. 7.08]
3. *F* [p. 7.09]
4. *F* [p. 7.09]
5. *T* [p. 7.10]
6. *F* [p. 7.12]
7. *F* [p. 7.14]
8. *F* [p. 7.17]
9. *T* [p. 7.22]
10. *T* [p. 7.27]

Multiple Choice

1. *b* [p. 7.05]
2. *b* [p. 7.06]
3. *c* [p. 7.08]
4. *a* [p. 7.09]
5. *d* [p. 7.12]
6. *d* [p. 7.13]
7. *b* [p. 7.15]
8. *a* [p. 7.19]
9. *d* [p. 7.21]
10. *d* [p. 7.30]

Fill in the Blanks

1. *volatile memory* [p. 7.02]
2. *Formatting* [p. 7.08]
3. *backup* [p. 7.09]
4. *Zip® disk* [p. 7.10]
5. *fixed disk* [p. 7.10]
6. *head crash* [p. 7.12]
7. *ATA* [p. 7.13]
8. *erasable CD* or *CD-E* [p. 7.22]
9. DVD writer [p. 7.25]
10. *computer output microfilm (COM) recorder* [p. 7.30]

Complete the Table

CHARACTERISTICS OF A 3.5-INCH HIGH DENSITY FLOPPY DISK

Capacity	*1.44 MB*
Number of sides	*2*
Tracks	80
Sectors per track	*18*
Bytes per sector	512
Sectors per disk	*2880*

Things to Think About

Answers will vary.

Puzzle Answer

Storage

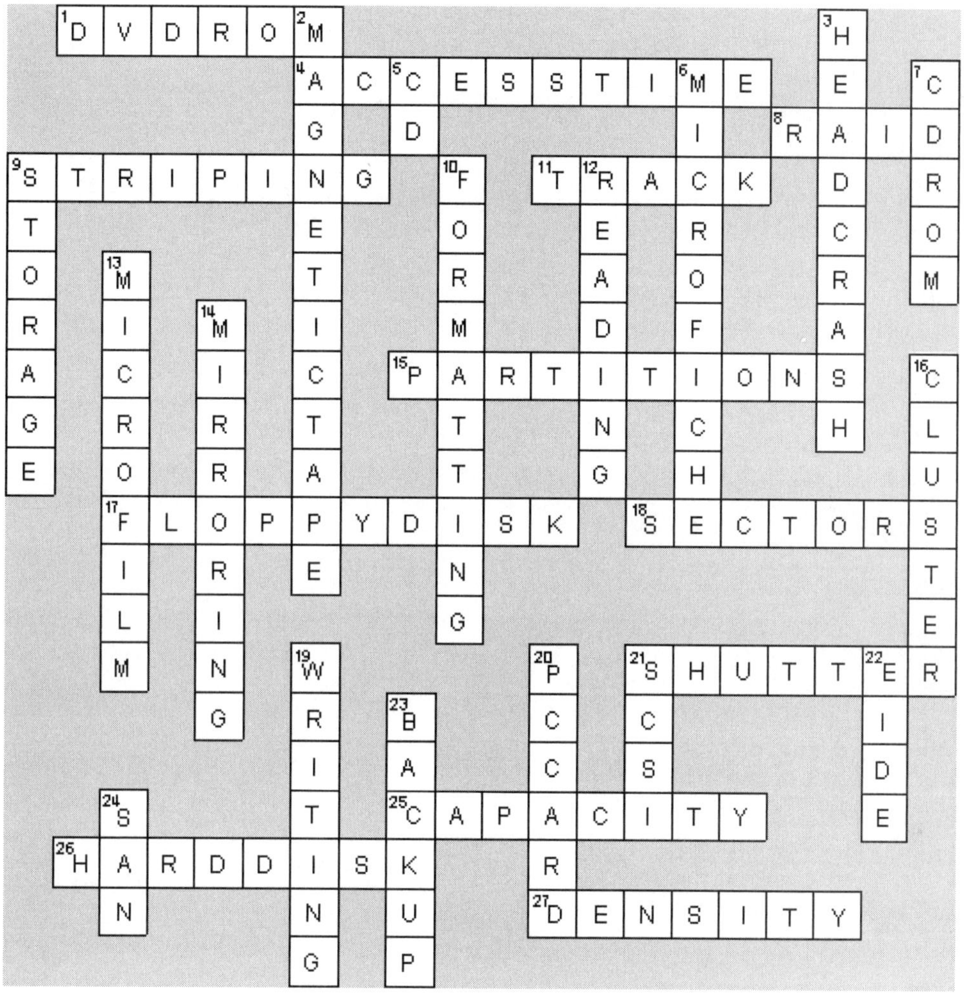

NOTES

DISCOVERING COMPUTERS 2003

STUDY GUIDE

CHAPTER 8

Operating Systems and Utility Programs

Chapter Overview

This chapter defines an operating system and discusses the functions common to most operating systems. You explore a variety of stand-alone operating systems, network operating systems, and embedded operating systems. Finally, the chapter describes several utility programs used with today's personal computers.

Chapter Objectives

After completing this chapter, you should be able to:

- Describe the two types of software
- Understand the startup process for a personal computer
- Describe the term user interface
- Explain features common to most operating systems
- Know the difference between stand-alone operating systems and network operating systems
- Identify various stand-alone operating systems
- Identify various network operating systems
- Recognize devices that use embedded operating systems
- Discuss the purpose of the following utilities: file viewer, file compression, diagnostic, uninstaller, disk scanner, disk defragmenter, backup, and screen saver

Chapter Outline

I. System software [p. 8.02]

System software consists of ____

____

II. Operating systems [p. 8.03]

An operating system (OS) is ____

____

The operating system sometimes is called the software platform or platform.

A cross-platform application is ____

____

III. Operating system functions [p. 8.04]

Most operating systems provide similar functions.

A. Starting a computer [p. 8.04]

Booting is ____

____

- A cold boot is ______________________________
- A warm boot is ______________________________

The kernel is ____

____

____

The kernel is a memory-resident program, which means ______________

____

Steps in a cold boot using the Windows XP operating system:

1. ____

   ____

2. ____

   ____

   The BIOS is ______________________________

3. ____

   ____

   The POST check ______________________________

   ____

4. ____

   ____

5. ____

   ____

   System files are ______________________________

6. ____

   ____

7. ____

   ____

   The registry consists ______________________________

   ____

The StartUp folder contains ______________________________

____

1. Recovery disk [p. 8.06]

   A boot drive is ____

   ____

   A recovery disk is ____

   ____

B. The user interface [p. 8.07]

A user interface controls ____

____

Types of user interfaces:

- With a command-line interface, you type ______________________________

  ____

  A command language is ____
- A graphical user interface (GUI) allows ______________________________

  ____

  A menu is ____

  An icon is ____

C. Managing programs [p. 8.08]

- A single user/single tasking operating system allows ____________________

  ____
- A multitasking operating system allows ______________________________

  ____

  The foreground contains ____

  The background contains ____
- A multiuser operating system enables ______________________________

  ____
- A multiprocessing operating system can support ____________________

  ____

  A fault-tolerant computer continues ______________________________

  ____

D. Managing memory [p. 8.10]

The purpose of memory management is ______________________________

____

With virtual memory (VM), the operating system allocates ____________________

____

- A swap file is ____
- A page is ____

- Paging is ______________________________
- Thrashing is ______________________________

E. Scheduling jobs [p. 8.10]

A job is ______________________________

A buffer is ______________________________

Spooling is ______________________________

____

Multiple print jobs line up in a queue.

A print spooler intercepts ______________________________

F. Configuring devices [p. 8.11]

A device driver is ______________________________

____

Plug and Play means ______________________________

____

An interrupt request (IRQ) is ______________________________

____

G. Accessing the Web [p. 8.13]

Operating systems typically provide a means to establish Web connections.

Some operating systems include a Web browser and an e-mail program.

H. Monitoring performance [p. 8.14]

A performance monitor is ______________________________

____

I. Providing housekeeping services [p. 8.14]

A file manager performs ______________________________

____

Formatting is ______________________________

The file allocation table (FAT) is ______________________________

____

J. Controlling a network [8.15]

A network is ______________________________

____

A network operating system is ______________________________

____

The server is ______________________________

Clients are ______________________________

K. Administering security [p. 8.16]

To log on, or access, a network, you must have a user name and password.

- A user name is ________________________________
- A password is ________________________________

Active Directory (AD) is ________________________________

____

IV. Types of operating systems [p. 8.17]

Many early operating systems were device dependent and proprietary, but the trend today is towards device-independent operating systems.

- Device-dependent software runs ________________________________

  ____

  Proprietary software is ________________________________
- Device-independent operating systems run ________________________________

  ____

New versions of an operating system usually are downward-compatible.

- A downward-compatible operating system is ________________________________

  ____
- An upward-compatible product is ________________________________

  ____

V. Stand-alone operating systems [p. 8.17]

A stand-alone operating system is ________________________________

____

Client operating systems work ________________________________

____

A. DOS [p. 8.17]

DOS refers ________________________________

____

Developed by Microsoft, DOS used a command-line interface. At one time, DOS was a widely used operating system.

B. Windows 3.x [p. 8.18]

Windows 3.x refers ________________________________

____

Windows 3.x actually is an operating environment, not an operating system. An operating environment is ________________________________

____

C. Windows 95 [p. 8.18]

Microsoft's Windows 95 is ______________________________

____

Advantages of Windows 95: ______________________________

____

____

D. Windows NT Workstation [p. 8.18]

Windows NT Workstation was developed ______________________________

____

Windows NT was ______________________________

E. Windows 98 [p. 8.18]

Microsoft's Windows 98 was ______________________________

____

Windows 98 included Internet Explorer, Windows Explorer, and an Active Desktop™.

- Internet Explorer is ______________________________
- Windows Explorer is ______________________________
- The Active Desktop™ interface allowed ______________________________

  ____

Windows 98 provided ______________________________

____

____

F. Windows 2000 Professional [p. 8.18]

Windows 2000 Professional is ______________________________

____

Features of Windows 2000 Professional included ______________________________

____

____

G. Windows Millennium Edition [p. 8.18]

Windows Millennium Edition is ______________________________

____

Windows Me allowed ______________________________

____

____

H. Windows XP [p. 8.19]

Windows XP is ______________________________

____

Windows XP is available in two editions.

1. Windows XP Home Edition [p. 8.20]

   The Windows XP Home Edition is ______________________________

   ____

   Windows XP Home Edition offers ______________________________

   ____

   ____

2. Windows XP Professional Edition [p. 8.20]

   The Windows XP Professional Edition is ______________________________

   ____

   Windows XP Professional Edition provides ______________________________

   ____

   ____

I. Mac OS [p. 8.21]

Apple's Macintosh operating system was ______________________________

____

Mac OS X is ______________________________

Features of the Mac OS X include ______________________________

____

J. OS/2 Warp Client [p. 8.22]

OS/2 Warp Client is ______________________________

____

VI. Network operating systems [p. 8.22]

A network operating system supports a network.

A. NetWare [p. 8.22]

NetWare is ______________________________

____

B. Windows NT Server [p. 8.22]

Windows NT Server was ______________________________

____

C. Windows 2000 Server [p. 8.22]

The Windows 2000 Server family consists of three products:

- Windows 2000 Server is ______________________________

  ____

- Windows 2000 Advanced Server is ______________________________

  ____

- Windows 2000 Datacenter Server is______________________________

  ____

D. Windows .NET Server [p. 8.22]

Windows .NET Server is______________________________________

____

E. OS/2 Warp Server for E-business [p. 8.23]

OS/2 Warp Server for E-business is ______________________________

____

F. UNIX [p. 8.23]

UNIX is ____

____

____

UNIX is a multipurpose operating system because ____________________

____

G. Linux [p. 8.24]

Linux is ____

____

Linux is open source software, which means ____________________

____

H. Solaris [p. 8.25]

Solaris™ is ____

____

VII. Embedded operating systems [p. 8.25]

An embedded operating system resides ______________________________

____

A. Windows CE [p. 8.25]

Windows CE is ____

____

The Auto PC is ____

B. Pocket PC 2002 [p. 8.26]

Pocket PC 2002 is ____

____

C. Palm OS [p. 8.26]

Palm OS® is ______________________________

____

VIII. Utility programs [p. 8.27]

A utility program is ______________________________

____

- Utility suites combine ______________________________
- A Web-based utility service allows ______________________________

____

A. File viewer [p. 8.27]

A file viewer ______________________________

____

Picture and Fax Viewer displays ______________________________

B. File compression [p. 8.28]

A file compression utility shrinks ______________________________

____

Compressed files, sometimes called zipped files, usually have a .zip extension. When you uncompress, or unzip, a file, you restore it to its original form.

C. Diagnostic utility [p. 8.28]

A diagnostic utility compiles ______________________________

____

Dr. Watson diagnoses ______________________________

D. Uninstaller [p. 8.29]

An uninstaller is ______________________________

____

E. Disk scanner [p. 8.29]

A disk scanner is a utility that:

(1) detects ______________________________

(2) searches ______________________________

F. Disk defragmenter [p. 8.30]

A disk defragmenter ______________________________

____

A fragmented file is ______________________________

Defragmenting reorganizes ______________________________

____

G. Backup utility [p. 8.30]

A backup utility allows ____

____

A restore program reverses ____

H. Screen saver [p. 8.31]

A screen saver is ____

____

Self Test

Matching

1. ____ utility suite
2. ____ file viewer
3. ____ file compression utility
4. ____ diagnostic utility
5. ____ uninstaller
6. ____ disk scanner
7. ____ disk defragmenter
8. ____ backup utility
9. ____ restore program
10. ____ screen saver

a. reverses the backup process and returns backed up files to their original form
b. utility that permanently etches images on a monitor screen
c. combines several utility programs into a single package
d. reduces the size of a file so it takes up less storage space than the original file
e. utility that detects and corrects disk problems and searches for and removes unwanted files
f. utility that causes the screen to display a moving image after a period of inactivity
g. utility that allows you to display and copy the contents of a file
h. compiles technical information about a computer's hardware and prepares a report
i. copies selected files, or the entire hard disk, onto another disk or tape
j. utility that removes an application, as well as associated entries in the system files
k. utility that locates, indexes, and loads system configuration information
l. utility that reorganizes files and unused space on a computer's hard disk

True/False

____ 1. In Windows, you can perform a warm boot by pressing a combination of keyboard keys, selecting options from a menu, or pressing the Reset button.

____ 2. During the boot process, if the system files are not on a disk in drive A, the BIOS looks in drive C (the designation usually given to the first hard disk).

____ 3. With a multitasking operating system, the application you currently are working on is in the background, and the others that are running but not being used are in the foreground.

____ 4. To stop thrashing, you should quit the application that stopped responding.

____ 5. With spooling, multiple print jobs are queued, or lined up, in the buffer.

____ 6. If you add a new device to your computer, such as a printer, its driver must be installed before the device will be operational.

____ 7. The disadvantage of device-independent operating systems is that if you change computer models or vendors, you cannot retain existing application software files and data files.

____ 8. Today, DOS is widely used because it offers a graphical user interface and can take full advantage of modern 32-bit microprocessors.

____ 9. Because only one version exists, UNIX provides interoperability across multiple platforms.

____ 10. When the contents of a file are gathered across two or more contiguous sectors on a disk, the file is fragmented.

Multiple Choice

____ 1. What is the drive from which your computer starts (usually drive C — the hard disk) called?
   a. the start drive
   b. the registry drive
   c. the boot drive
   d. the BIOS drive

____ 2. Today, what are most operating systems?
   a. single user/single tasking
   b. multitasking
   c. multiuser
   d. multiprocessing

____ 3. Buffers, swap files, pages, paging, and thrashing all are terms related to what basic function of an operating system?
   a. managing memory
   b. configuring devices
   c. monitoring system performance
   d. administering security

____ 4. What is the program that manages and intercepts print jobs and places them in the queue called?
   a. the print driver
   b. the print spooler
   c. the print buffer
   d. the print saver

____ 5. Which of the following was *not* an operating system, but instead was an operating environment for DOS?
   a. Windows 3.x
   b. Windows 95
   c. Windows 98
   d. Windows NT

____ 6. What popular Web browser was included with Windows 98?
   a. Windows Explorer
   b. NetWare
   c. Internet Explorer
   d. Netscape Navigator

____ 7. What multitasking operating system is available only for computers manufactured by Apple?
   a. Linux
   b. UNIX
   c. Windows 98
   d. Mac OS X

____ 8. What is a weakness of UNIX?
   a. it is a single user/single tasking operating system, and no versions are available for most computers
   b. it is incapable of handling a high volume of transactions or working with multiple processors using multiprocessing
   c. it has a command-line interface, and many of its commands are difficult to remember and use
   d. all of the above

____ 9. Dr. Watson is an example of what type of utility?
   a. a diagnostic utility
   b. a disk scanner
   c. a disk defragmenter
   d. a file compression utility

____ 10. A restore program generally is included with what type of utility?
   a. a screen saver
   b. an uninstaller utility
   c. a file viewer
   d. a backup utility

Fill in the Blanks

1. Parts of an operating system are ____________________, which means their instructions remain on the hard disk until they are needed.
2. If the POST completes successfully, the BIOS searches for specific operating system files called ____________________.
3. A(n) ____________________ continues to operate even if one of its components fails.
4. An operating system is ____________________ if it spends much of its time paging, instead of executing application software.
5. Multiple print jobs line up in a(n) ____________________ within the buffer.
6. A program called a(n) ____________________ intercepts print jobs from the operating system and places them in the queue.

7. A(n) ____________________ is an icon on the desktop that runs a program when you click it.
8. Microsoft developed ____________________ to meet the need for an operating system that had a GUI.
9. Compressed files, sometimes called ____________________, usually have a .zip extension.
10. Screen savers were developed to prevent a problem called ____________________, in which images could be permanently etched on a monitor's screen.

Complete the Table

CATEGORIES OF OPERATING SYSTEMS

Stand-alone	• DOS	• ____________________
	• ____________________	• Windows XP Professional Edition
	• Windows 95	• ____________________
	• ____________________	• OS/2 Warp Client
	• Windows 98	• ____________________
	• ____________________	• Linux
	• Windows Millennium Edition	
__________	• ____________________	• OS/2 Warp Server for E-business
	• Windows NT Server	• ____________________
	• ____________________	• Linux
	• Windows XP Server	• ____________________
Embedded	• Windows CE	• ____________________
	• ____________________	

Things to Think About

1. How has the concept of user-friendly (being easy to learn and use) affected the development of operating systems? What operating systems seem the most, and least, user-friendly? Why?
2. Why is a boot disk important? In Windows, how can you create a boot disk?
3. What three functions of an operating system are most important for a home computer user? For an office computer user? Why?
4. From most important to least important, how would you rank the utility programs described in this chapter? Why did you rank the programs as you did?

Puzzle

The terms described by the phrases below are written below each line in code. Break the code by writing the correct term above the coded word. Then, use your broken code to translate the final sentence.

1. Consists of the programs that control the operations of the computer and its devices — ______ OUOPAI OKBPSWNA
2. A set of programs containing instructions that coordinate all of the activities among hardware — ______ KLANWPEJC OUOPAI
3. The core of an operating system — ______ GANJAH
4. The part of the software with which you interact — ______ QOAN EJPANBWYA
5. Displays a set of available commands or options from which you can choose — ______ IAJQ
6. A small image that represents an item such as a program, an instruction, or a file — ______ EYKJ
7. Operating system capability that allows a user to work on two or more applications that reside in memory — ______ IQHPEPWOGEJC
8. Allocates a portion of a storage medium to function as additional RAM — ______ RENPQWH IAIKNU
9. What happens when an operating system spends too much time paging instead of executing software — ______ PDNWODEJC
10. Small program that converts commands into instructions a hardware device understands — ______ ZNERAN
11. A communications line between a device and the CPU — ______ EJPANNQLP NAMQAOP
12. Combination of characters associated with a user name that allows access to certain computer resources — ______ LWOOSKNZ
13. Program that performs functions related to storage and file management — ______ BEHA IWJWCAN
14. Turning on a computer after it has been powered off completely — ______ YKHZ XKKP
15. Several files in which the system configuration information is contained — ______ NACEOPNU
16. Floppy disk that contains certain operating system commands that will start the computer — ______ XKKP ZEOG

17. A type of system software that performs a specific task, usually related to managing a computer ______________ QPEHEPU LNKCNWI

18. Compressed files, usually with a .zip extension ______________ VELLAZ BEHAO

19. What you do to restore a zipped file to its original form ______________ QJYKILNAOO

20. Windows utility that reorganizes a disk so files are stored in contiguous sectors ______________ ZEOG ZABNWCIAJPAN

____

W LNKCNWI YWHHAZ OUOPAI YKIIWJZAN ZAHQTA IWGAO

____

YDKKOEJC WJ KLANWPEJC OUOPAI AWOEAN XU AHEIEJWPEJC PDA

____

JAAZ PK IWGA W YDKEYA, WHHKSEJC QOANO PK OSEPYD AWOEHU

____

WIKJC QL PK PDENPU-PSK ZEBBANAJP KLANWPEJC OUOPAIO.

Self Test Answers

Matching

1. *c* [p. 8.27]
2. *g* [p. 8.27]
3. *d* [p. 8.28]
4. *h* [p. 8.28]
5. *j* [p. 8.29]
6. *e* [p. 8.29]
7. *l* [p. 8.30]
8. *i* [p. 8.30]
9. *a* [p. 8.30]
10. *f* [p. 8.31]

True/False

1. *T* [p. 8.04]
2. *T* [p. 8.06]
3. *F* [p. 8.09]
4. *T* [p. 8.10]
5. *T* [p. 8.11]
6. *T* [p. 8.12]
7. *F* [p. 8.17]
8. *F* [p. 8.18]
9. *F* [p. 8.23]
10. *F* [p. 8.30]

Multiple Choice

1. *c* [p. 8.06]
2. *b* [p. 8.08]
3. *a* [p. 8.10]
4. *b* [p. 8.11]
5. *a* [p. 8.18]
6. *c* [p. 8.18]
7. *d* [p. 8.21]
8. *c* [p. 8.23]
9. *a* [p. 8.28]
10. *d* [p. 8.30]

Fill in the Blanks

1. *nonresident* [p. 8.04]
2. *system files* [p. 8.06]
3. *fault-tolerant computer* [p. 8.09]
4. *thrashing* [p. 8.10]
5. *queue* [p. 8.11]
6. *print spooler* [p. 8.11]
7. *shortcut* [p. 8.14]
8. *Windows* [p. 8.18]
9. *zipped files* [p. 8.28]
10. *ghosting* [p. 8.31]

Complete the Table

CATEGORIES OF OPERATING SYSTEMS

Stand-alone	• DOS	• *Windows XP Home Edition*
	• *Windows 3.x*	• Windows XP Professional Edition
	• Windows 95	• *Mac OS X*
	• *Windows NT Workstation*	• OS/2 Warp Client
	• Windows 98	• *UNIX*
	• *Windows 2000 Professional*	• Linux
	• Windows Millennium Edition	
Network	• *NetWare*	• OS/2 Warp Server for E-business
	• Windows NT Server	• *UNIX*
	• *Windows 2000 Server*	• Linux
	• Windows XP Server	• *Solaris*
Embedded	• Windows CE	• *Palm OS*
	• *Pocket PC 2002*	

Things to Think About

Answers will vary.

Puzzle Answer

1.	Consists of the programs that control the operations of the computer and its devices	*system software* OUOPAI OKBPSWNA
2.	A set of programs containing instructions that coordinate all of the activities among hardware	*operating system* KLANWPEJC OUOPAI
3.	The core of an operating system	*kernel* GANJAH
4.	The part of the software with which you interact	*user interface* QOAN EJPANBWYA
5.	Displays a set of available commands or options from which you can choose	*menu* IAJQ
6.	A small image that represents an item such as a program, an instruction, or a file	*icon* EYKJ
7.	Operating system capability that allows a user to work on two or more applications that reside in memory	*multitasking* IQHPEPWOGEJC
8.	Allocates a portion of a storage medium to function as additional RAM	*virtual memory* RENPQWH IAIKNU
9.	What happens when an operating system spends too much time paging instead of executing software	*thrashing* PDNWODEJC
10.	Small program that converts commands into instructions a hardware device understands	*driver* ZNERAN
11.	A communications line between a device and the CPU	*interrupt request* EJPANNQLP NAMQAOP
12.	Combination of characters associated with a user name that allows access to certain computer resources	*password* LWOOSKNZ
13.	Program that performs functions related to storage and file management	*file manager* BEHA IWJWCAN
14.	Turning on a computer after it has been powered off completely	*cold boot* YKHZ XKKP
15.	Several files in which the system configuration information is contained	*registry* NACEOPNU
16.	Floppy disk that contains certain operating system commands that will start the computer	*boot disk* XKKP ZEOG
17.	A type of system software that performs a specific task, usually related to managing a computer	*utility program* QPEHEPU LNKCNWI

18. Compressed files, usually with a .zip extension — *zipped files*
VELLAZ BEHAO

19. What you do to restore a zipped file to its original form — *uncompress*
QJYKILNAOO

20. Windows utility that reorganizes a disk so files are stored in contiguous sectors — *Disk Defragmenter*
ZEOG ZABNWCIAJPAN

A program called System Commander Deluxe makes
W LNKCNWI YWHHAZ OUOPAI YKIIWJZAN ZAHQTA IWGAO

choosing an operating system easier by eliminating the
YDKKOEJC WJ KLANWPEJC OUOPAI AWOEAN XU AHEIEJWPEJC PDA

need to make a choice, allowing users to switch easily
JAAZ PK IWGA W YDKEYA, WHHKSEJC QOANO PK OSEPYD AWOEHU

among up to thirty-two different operating systems.
WIKJC QL PK PDENPU-PSK ZEBBANAJP KLANWPEJC OUOPAIO.

NOTES

DISCOVERING COMPUTERS 2003

STUDY GUIDE

CHAPTER 9

Communications and Networks

Chapter Overview

This chapter provides an overview of communications terminology and applications. You learn how computers can be joined together into a network, allowing them to communicate and share resources such as hardware, software, data, and information. The chapter also explains various communications devices, media, and procedures as they relate to computers.

Chapter Objectives

After completing this chapter, you should be able to:

- Define the components required for successful communications
- Identify various sending and receiving devices
- Explain communications applications
- List advantages of using a network
- Differentiate between a local area network and a wide area network
- Understand the various communications technologies
- Identify uses of intranets and extranets
- Explain the purpose of communications software
- Understand the telephone network
- Describe commonly used communications devices
- Identify various physical and wireless transmission media

Chapter Outline

I. Communications [p. 9.02]

Computer communications describes ______________________________

____

For successful communications, you need:

- A sending device that initiates ______________________________

  ____

- A communications device that converts data from the sending device into signals that can be carried by a communications channel.

- A communications channel, or path, on which the signals travel.
- A communications device that receives signals from the communications channel and converts them so they can be understood by the receiving device.
- A receiving device that accepts ______________________________

____

A communications device, such as a modem, converts between the digital signal used by a computer and the analog signal suitable for a communications channel.

- An analog signal consists ______________________________
- A digital signal consists ______________________________

II. Sending and receiving devices [p. 9.03]

Various types of computers serve as sending and receiving devices. Internet appliances and Web-enabled devices also serve as sending and receiving devices. An Internet appliance is ______________________________

____

A Web-enabled device is ______________________________

____

III. Uses of communications technologies [p. 9.04]

A. Voice mail [p. 9.04]

Voice mail allows ______________________________

A voice mailbox is ______________________________

B. Fax [p. 9.05]

A fax can contain ______________________________

____

C. E-mail [p. 9.05]

E-mail (electronic mail) is ______________________________

____

D. Instant messaging [p. 9.06]

Instant messaging (IM) is ______________________________

____

E. Chat rooms [p. 9.06]

A chat room permits ______________________________

____

- Voice chats and video chats let you hear ______________________________

  ____

- Radio chats play ______________________________

F. Newsgroups [p. 9.07]

A newsgroup is ______________________________

____

G. Telephony [p. 9.08]

Internet telephony enables ______________________________

____

Internet telephone software digitizes ______________________________

____

H. Videoconferencing [p. 9.08]

A videoconference involves ______________________________

____

I. Collaboration [p. 9.09]

Many communications software products provide a means to collaborate with, or work with, other users connected to a server.

An online meeting allows ______________________________

____

J. Groupware [p. 9.10]

Groupware is ______________________________

____

K. Global positioning system [p. 9.10]

A global positioning system (GPS) consists ______________________________

____

IV. Networks [p. 9.11]

A network is ______________________________

____

Advantages of using a network:

- Facilitating communications — ______________________________

  ____

- Sharing hardware — ______________________________

  ____

- Sharing data and information — ______________________________

  ____

- Sharing software — ______________________________

  ____

  A site license is ______________________________

A virtual private network (VPN) provides ______________________________

____

A. Local area network (LAN) [p. 9.12]

A local area network (LAN) is ______________________________

____

A wireless LAN (WLAN) is ______________________________

A network operating system (NOS) is ______________________________

____

Tasks performed by a NOS:

- Administration — ______________________________
- File management — ______________________________
- Printer management — ______________________________
- Security — ______________________________

Two types of LANs are peer-to-peer and client/server.

1. Peer-to-peer [p. 9.13]

   A peer-to-peer LAN is ______________________________

   ____

2. Client/server [p. 9.14]

   A client/server LAN is ______________________________

   ____

   - A server controls ______________________________

     ____

     Dedicated servers perform ______________________________

     - A file server stores ______________________________
     - A print server manages ______________________________
     - A database server stores ______________________________
     - A network server manages ______________________________

   - Clients rely ______________________________

     ____

   A network administrator is ______________________________

   ____

B. Wide area network (WAN) [p. 9.15]

A wide area network (WAN) is ______________________________

____

The Internet is the world's largest WAN.

1. Internet peer-to-peer [p. 9.16]
   P2P describes ______________________________

   ____

C. Metropolitan area network (MAN) [p. 9.16]
   A metropolitan area network (MAN) is ______________________________

   ____

D. Network topologies [p. 9.16]
   A network topology is ______________________________

   ____

   Commonly used network topologies:

   1. Bus network [p. 9.17]
      A bus network consists ______________________________

      ____

      The bus is ______________________________
   2. Ring network [p. 9.17]
      In a ring network, a cable forms ______________________________

      ____
   3. Star network [p. 9.18]
      In a star network, all devices connect ______________________________

      ____

      The hub is ______________________________

E. Network communications technologies [p. 9.18]
   1. Ethernet [p. 9.18]
      Ethernet is ______________________________

      ____

      - Fast Ethernet transmits ______________________________
      - Gigabit Ethernet provides ______________________________
   2. Token ring [p. 9.19]
      Token ring controls ______________________________

      ____
   3. TCP/IP [p. 9.19]
      TCP/IP (Transmission control protocol/Internet protocol) is ______________________________

      ____

      - Packets are ______________________________
      - Routers are ______________________________
      - Packet switching is ______________________________

4. 802.11 specification [p. 9.20]

   802.11 is ______________________________

   Windows XP supports 802.11b, which is a popular 802.11 specification.

5. WAP [p. 9.20]

   Wireless Application Protocol (WAP) allows ______________________________

   ____

   WAP-enabled devices include ______________________________

F. Intranets [p. 9.20]

An intranet is ______________________________

____

An extranet allows ______________________________

____

1. Firewalls [p. 9.21]

   A firewall is ______________________________

   ____

G. Home networks [p. 9.22]

A home network connects ______________________________

____

Types of home networks:

- An Ethernet network requires a cable to connect each computer.
- A HomePLC (powerline cable) network is ______________________________

  ____
- A phoneline network is ______________________________

  ____
- A HomeRF (radio frequency) network uses ______________________________

  ____

An intelligent home network extends ______________________________

____

V. Communications software [p. 9.23]

Communications software consists ______________________________

____

FTP (file transfer protocol) is ______________________________

____

- An FTP server is ______________________________
- Anonymous FTP allows ______________________________

VI. The telephone network [p. 9.25]

The public switched telephone network (PSTN) is ______________________________

____

Data can be sent over the telephone network using dial-up lines or dedicated lines.

A. Dial-up lines [p. 9.25]

A dial-up line is ____

____

B. Dedicated lines [p. 9.25]

A dedicated line is ____

____

A transfer rate is ____

Transfer rates usually are expressed as bits per second (bps) — that is, the number of bits the line can transmit in one second.

Popular types of dedicated lines are ISDN lines, DSL, T-carrier lines, and ATM.

C. ISDN lines [p. 9.26]

ISDN (Integrated Services Digital Network) is ___________________________

____

Multiplexing is ____

D. DSL [p. 9.26]

DSL (digital subscriber line) transmits _____________________________

____

ADSL is ____

E. Cable television lines [p 9.26]

Although not a type of telephone line, cable television (CATV) lines are a type of dedicated line that allows home users to connect to the Internet.

F. T-carrier lines [p. 9.27]

A T-carrier line is ____

____

- A T1 line is ____
- A T3 line is ____

G. Asynchronous transfer mode [p. 9.27]

Asynchronous transfer mode (ATM) is ______________________________

____

VII. Communications devices [p. 9.27]

A communications device is ______________________________

____

A. Modems [p. 9.28]

A modem converts ______________________________

____

- An external modem is ______________________________

  ____

- An internal modem is ______________________________

  ____

- A wireless modem allows ______________________________

  ____

B. ISDN and DSL modems [p. 9.28]

A digital modem is ______________________________

____

- An ISDN modem sends ______________________________

  ____

- A DSL modem sends ______________________________

  ____

C. Cable modems [p. 9.29]

A cable modem is ______________________________

____

D. Network interface card [p. 9.29]

A network interface card (NIC) is ______________________________

____

E. Connecting networks [p. 9.30]

A hub is ______________________________

VIII. Communications channel [p. 9.31]

The channel is ______________________________

Bandwidth is ______________________________

Transmission media consists ______________________________

____

- Baseband media can transmit ______________________________
- Broadband media can transmit ______________________________

Transmission media are one of two types:

- Physical transmission media use ______________________________

  ____

- Wireless transmission media send ______________________________

  ____

IX. Physical transmission media [p. 9.32]

A. Twisted-pair cable [p. 9.33]

Twisted-pair cable consists ______________________________

____

- Each twisted-pair wire consists______________________________

  ____

  Wires are twisted to reduce noise, which is ______________________________

  ____

B. Coaxial cable [p. 9.33]

Coaxial cable (coax) consists ______________________________

____

____

C. Fiber-optic cable [p. 9.34]

Fiber-optic cable consists ______________________________

____

An optical fiber is ______________________________

Advantages of fiber-optic cable:

- ______________________________
- ______________________________
- ______________________________
- ______________________________
- ______________________________

Disadvantages of fiber-optic cable are that it costs more than twisted-pair or coaxial cable and can be difficult to install and modify.

X. Wireless transmission media [p. 9.34]

A. Broadcast radio [p. 9.34]

Broadcast radio is ______________________________

____

- Bluetooth™ uses ______________________________

  ____

B. Cellular radio [p. 9.36]

Cellular radio is ______________________________

____

- A cellular telephone is ______________________________

  ____

- Personal Communications Services (PCS) is ______________________________

  ____

- 3G provides ______________________________

C. Microwaves [p. 9.37]

Microwaves are ______________________________

____

- A microwave station is ______________________________

  ____

Microwaves use line-of-sight transmission, which means ______________________________

____

D. Communications satellite [p. 9.38]

A communications satellite is ______________________________

____

- An uplink is ______________________________
- A downlink is ______________________________

E. Infrared [p. 9.39]

Infrared is ______________________________

____

Self Test

Matching

1. ____ voice mail
2. ____ fax
3. ____ e-mail
4. ____ instant messaging
5. ____ chat room
6. ____ newsgroup
7. ____ Internet telephony
8. ____ videoconference
9. ____ groupware
10. ____ global positioning system

a. permits users to converse in real time via a computer while connected to the Internet
b. area on the Web where users conduct written discussions about a particular subject
c. real-time communications service that notifies you when one or more people are online
d. handheld device that provides access to the Internet from any location
e. includes activities such as shopping, banking, investing, and other uses of electronic money
f. consists of earth-based receivers that accept and analyze satellite signals to determine location
g. the exchange of text messages and computer files transmitted via a communications network
h. can contain handwritten or typed text, illustrations, photographs, or other graphics
i. involves using video and computer technology to conduct a meeting
j. functions like an answering machine, allowing callers to leave a voice message
k. software application that helps people work together and share information over a network
l. enables you to talk to other people over the Internet

True/False

____ 1. Sending and receiving devices convert or format signals so they are suitable for a communications channel.

____ 2. A chat room is asynchronous, while a newsgroup is synchronous.

____ 3. Internet telephone software expands a conversation (the audio) and then transmits the analog audio over the Internet to the called parties.

____ 4. Often, nodes (computers or devices) are connected to a LAN via cables.

____ 5. In a peer-to-peer network, the server contains both the network operating system and application software.

____ 6. Two examples of networking software that allow P2P are Napster and Gnutella.

____ 7. With TCP/IP, packets travel along the fastest available path to a recipient's computer via devices called routers.

____ 8. A HomePLC (powerline cable) network requires additional wiring.

____ 9. According to the definition of a modem (to convert from analog to digital signals and vice versa), the use of the term modem in the context of a digital modem is not correct.

____ 10. Most of today's computer networks use coaxial cable because other transmission media transmit signals at slower rates.

Multiple Choice

____ 1. On what type of computers do people use IM (instant messaging)?
   a. desktop computers
   b. notebook computers
   c. Web-enabled handheld computers and devices
   d. all of the above

____ 2. What simple, inexpensive network typically connects less than 10 computers together?
   a. a peer-to-peer WAN
   b. a client/server WAN
   c. a peer-to-peer LAN
   d. a client/server LAN

____ 3. What type of dedicated server manages printers and print jobs?
   a. a network server
   b. a file server
   c. a print server
   d. a database server

____ 4. What type of dedicated server manages network traffic?
   a. a network server
   b. a file server
   c. a print server
   d. a database server

____ 5. What communications technology commonly is used for Internet transmissions?
   a. TCP/IP
   b. token ring
   c. Ethernet
   d. WAP (Wireless Application Protocol)

____ 6. With ISDN, the same telephone line that could carry only one computer signal, now can carry three or more signals at once using what technique?
   a. modulating
   b. routing
   c. multiplexing
   d. receiving

____ 7. What type of modem typically uses the same waves used by cellular telephones?
   a. an internal modem
   b. a wireless modem
   c. an external modem
   d. a digital modem

____ 8. What do personal computers on a LAN typically contain?
   a. a DSL (digital subscriber line)
   b. a PCS (personal communications service)
   c. a TCP (transmission control protocol)
   d. a NIC (network interface card)

____ 9. Many local and long-distance telephone companies and cable television operators are replacing existing telephone and coaxial cable with what?
   a. broadcast radio
   b. twisted-pair cable
   c. cellular radio
   d. fiber-optic cable

____ 10. What is used by applications such as air navigation, television and radio broadcast, videoconferencing, paging, and global positioning systems?
   a. coaxial cable
   b. communications satellites
   c. infrared
   d. microwaves

Fill in the Blanks

1. A voice mail system usually provides an individual ____________________ for each user, which can be accessed to listen to messages.
2. A(n) ____________________ is a conferencing system that uses the Internet, Web browsers, and Web servers to deliver a videoconferencing service.
3. Home users today can make a(n) ____________________, where both parties see each other as they talk on the Internet.
4. Groupware is a component of a broad concept called ____________________, which includes network hardware and software that enables group members to communicate, manage projects, schedule meetings, and make group decisions.
5. A computer chip, called ____________________, can be worn on a bracelet or chain and has an antenna that communicates with a GPS satellite.

6. A(n) ____________________ is a dedicated server that stores and manages files.
7. A(n) ____________________ is a dedicated server that stores and provides access to a database.
8. Transfer rates can be thousands of bits per second, called ____________________.
9. The word modem is derived from the words ____________________, to change to an analog signal, and ____________________, to convert back to a digital signal.
10. Some networks use a(n) ____________________, which both sends and receives signals from wireless devices.

Complete the Table

SPEEDS OF VARIOUS CONNECTIONS TO THE INTERNET

Type of Line	Transfer Rates	Approximate Monthly Cost
____________	Up to 56 Kbps	Local or long-distance rates
ISDN (BRI)	____________	$10 to $40
ADSL	128 Kbps – 9 Mbps	____________
Cable TV (CATV)	128 Kbps – 2.5 Mbps	____________
____________	1.544 Mbps	$1,000 or more
T3	____________	$10,000 or more
____________	155 Mbps to 622 Mbps	____________

Things to Think About

1. What two uses of communications technologies have had the greatest impact on personal interactions? What uses have had the greatest impact on business interactions? Why?
2. What network capability — hardware sharing, data and information sharing, software sharing, or facilitated communications — would be most important to a school? To a business? To a government office? Why?
3. What network topology — bus, ring, or star — would be best for a school? For a business? For a government office? Why?
4. What might be the advantages of connecting multiple computers in your home in a home network? Which type of home network would you use? Why?

Puzzle

All of the words described below appear in the puzzle. Words may be either forward or backward, across, up and down, or diagonal. Circle each word as you find it.

Communications and Networks

```
      M     Y L M     S
    O   O   S   P   I   F
    C     D   M   T     Q
      N A   U U E   F Y
              L
D K S T Z I I T A H N O I S E
O R U R S C P I N T Z P F C R
W O B A E H B P A O E E N I A
N W A N X A F L L O S E A S W
L T S S T T E E O T R R M D P
I E E F H R T X G E M T M N U
N N B E G O A I F U L O I A O
K I A R I O R N P L I P C B R
R L N R S M O G S B A E R D G
E P D A F C B K T C M E O A S
V U W T O B A N N M E R W O W
R L I E E U L I E E C I A R E
E A D B N H L L I D I N V B N
S I T P I H O P L O O G E E E
V D H S L X C U C M V L S H R
```

Type of signal that consists of a continuous electrical wave

Allows callers to leave a voice message for the called party

Can contain handwritten or typed text, illustrations, or graphics

The exchange of text messages and computer files via a network

Permits users to converse in real time via a computer connected to the Internet

Areas on the Web where users conduct written discussions on a topic

Involves using video and computer technology to conduct a meeting

Work together with others connected to a server

Application that helps people work together on projects over a network

Collection of computers and devices connected by communications channels

Legal agreement that allows multiple users to run a software package simultaneously

Network that connects computers in a limited geographical area

System software that organizes and coordinates activities on a LAN

Simple, inexpensive type of LAN that connects less than 10 computers

Computers on a client/server LAN that rely on the server for resources

Controls access to the hardware and software on a client/server LAN

Backbone network that connects LANs in a city or town

Type of network that consists of a single cable to which all computers connect

Type of network with all computers arranged along a closed loop

Type of network in which all devices connect to a central computer

Internet standard that allows users to upload and download files

Worldwide telephone network that handles voice-oriented telephone calls

Temporary connection that uses one or more analog telephone lines

Speed at which a line carries data and information

The number of bits a communications line can transmit in one second

Set of standards for digital transmission of data over standard telephone lines

Technique that allows a telephone line to carry three or more signals at once

Type of DSL that supports faster transfer rates when receiving data

Communications device that converts between digital and analog signals

To change a digital signal into an analog signal

Device that provides a central point for cables in a network

Width of a communications channel, which affects quantity transmitted

Type of media that can transmit only one signal at a time

Type of media that can transmit multiple signals simultaneously

Electrical disturbance that can degrade communications

Both sends and receives signals from wireless devices on a network

Uses short-range radio waves to transmit data among enabled devices

Set of technologies used for completely digital cellular devices

Radio waves that provide a high-speed signal transmission

Transmission that must be in a straight line with no obstructions

Transmission from an earth-based station to a communications satellite

Transmission from a communications satellite to an earth-based station

Self Test Answers

Matching

1. *j* [p. 9.04]
2. *h* [p. 9.05]
3. *g* [p. 9.05]
4. *c* [p. 9.06]
5. *a* [p. 9.06]
6. *b* [p. 9.07]
7. *l* [p. 9.08]
8. *i* [p. 9.08]
9. *k* [p. 9.10]
10. *f* [p. 9.10]

True/False

1. *F* [p. 9.03]
2. *F* [p. 9.07]
3. *F* [p. 9.08]
4. *T* [p. 9.12]
5. *F* [p. 9.13]
6. *T* [p. 9.16]
7. *T* [p. 9.19]
8. *F* [p. 9.22]
9. *T* [p. 9.28]
10. *F* [p. 9.34]

Multiple Choice

1. *d* [p. 9.06]
2. *c* [p. 9.13]
3. *c* [p. 9.14]
4. *a* [p. 9.14]
5. *a* [p. 9.19]
6. *c* [p. 9.26]
7. *b* [p. 9.28]
8. *d* [p. 9.29]
9. *d* [p. 9.34]
10. *b* [p. 9.39]

Fill in the Blanks

1. *voice mailbox* [p. 9.04]
2. *Web conference* [p. 9.08]
3. *video telephone call* [p. 9.08]
4. *workgroup computing* [p. 9.10]
5. *Digital Angel™* [p. 9.11]
6. *file server* [p. 9.14]
7. *database server* [p. 9.14]
8. *kilobits per second (Kbps)* [p. 9.26]
9. *modulate/demodulate* [p. 9.28]
10. *transceiver* [p. 9.35]

Complete the Table

SPEEDS OF VARIOUS CONNECTIONS TO THE INTERNET

Type of Line	Transfer Rates	Approximate Monthly Cost
Dial-up	Up to 56 Kbps	Local or long-distance rates
ISDN (BRI)	*Up to 128 Kbps*	$10 to $40
ADSL	128 Kbps – 9 Mbps	*$40 to $80*
Cable TV (CATV)	128 Kbps – 2.5 Mbps	*$30 to $50*
T1	1.544 Mbps	$1,000 or more
T3	*44 Mbps*	$10,000 or more
ATM	155 Mbps to 622 Mbps	*$8,000 or more*

Things to Think About

Answers will vary.

Puzzle Answer

Communications and Networks

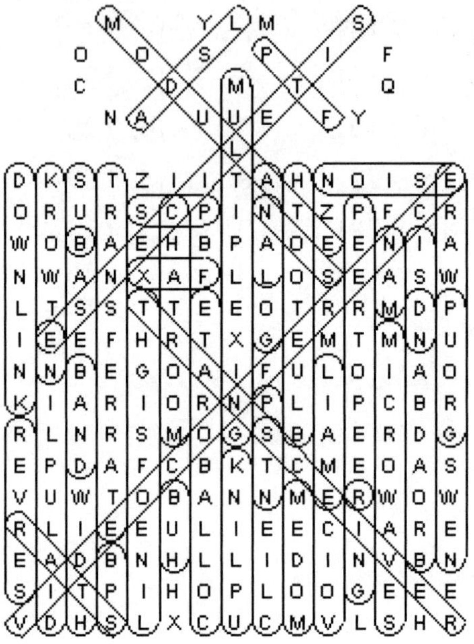

DISCOVERING COMPUTERS 2003

STUDY GUIDE

CHAPTER 10

E-Commerce

Chapter Overview

This chapter discusses how e-commerce has changed today's business practices. You learn about various e-commerce business models and revenue streams. Then, e-retailing and other market sectors are described. Finally, the chapter presents issues associated with building an electronic storefront, accepting payment, managing product delivery, designing a Web site, managing the Web site, and promoting the Web site.

Chapter Objectives

After completing this chapter, you should be able to:

- Understand how e-commerce has changed today's business practices
- Discuss the positive impact of e-commerce on global society
- Differentiate between the various e-commerce business models: business-to-consumer, consumer-to-consumer, business-to-business, and business-to-employee
- Identify various e-commerce revenue streams
- Know how e-retailing works
- Identify e-commerce market sectors
- Discuss issues associated with building an electronic storefront, accepting payment, managing product delivery, designing a Web site, managing the Web site, and promoting the Web site

Chapter Outline

I. What is e-commerce [p. 10.02]

E-commerce (electronic commerce) is ________________________________

____

M-commerce (mobile commerce) identifies ____________________________

____

- A bricks-and-mortar business is ____________________________

  ____

- A clicks-and-mortar business is ______________________________

____

A. The growth of e-commerce [p. 10.04]

Worldwide e-commerce exceeded $600 billion in the year 2001 and is expected to reach $5 trillion by 2004. Improvements in communications technologies and computing hardware and software have contributed to the phenomenal growth.

One of the first steps in the development of e-commerce was electronic data interchange. Electronic data interchange (EDI) is ______________________

____

II. E-commerce business models [p. 10.04]

E-commerce business can be grouped into four models: business-to-consumer, consumer-to-consumer, business-to-business, and business-to-employee.

A. Business-to-consumer e-commerce [p. 10.04]

Business-to-consumer (B2C or B-to-C) e-commerce consists ____________

____

With disintermediation, B2C businesses sell ______________________

____

B. Consumer-to-consumer e-commerce [p. 10.06]

Consumer-to-consumer (C2C or C-to-C) e-commerce consists ____________

____

Forms of C2C:

- An online auction is ______________________________

  ____

- P2P describes ______________________________

  ____

C. Business-to-business e-commerce [p. 10.06]

Business-to-business e-commerce (B2B or B-to-B) consists ____________

____

A supply chain is ______________________________

____

Basic types of B2B sites:

- A vendor B2B site is ______________________________

  ____

- A service B2B site uses ______________________________

____

- A brokering B2B site acts ______________________________

____

- An infomediary B2B site provides ______________________________

____

D. Business-to-employee e-commerce [p 10.08]

Business-to-employee (B2E or B-to-E) e-commerce refers ______________

____

An intranet is ______________________________

____

E. Advantages of e-commerce [p. 10.08]

Some of the advantages of e-commerce are:

- ______________ • ______________
- ______________ • ______________
- ______________ • ______________
- ______________ • ______________
- ______________ • ______________
- ______________

III. E-commerce revenue streams [p. 10.08]

A revenue stream is ______________________________

____

Common e-commerce revenue streams:

- Selling goods to consumers or to other businesses.
- Using electronic software distribution (ESD) to sell ______________

____

- Renting software. A Web application is ______________________________

____

- Generating revenues through advertisement.
- Hosting Web sites. A Web hosting service provides ______________

____

A Web server is ______________________________

- Offering online storage. Online storage services provide ______________

____

- Providing Internet access for a fee.

IV. The e-retailing market sector [p. 10.12]

E-retail occurs ______________________________

____

An electronic storefront is ______________________________

____

The shopping cart is ______________________________

____

V. Other e-commerce market sectors on the Web [p. 10.14]

In addition to retail, other market sectors take advantage of the Web.

A. Finance [p. 10.14]

Finance-related Web sites can include banks, mortgage firms, brokerage companies, and insurance companies.

- Online banking allows ______________________________

  ____

- Online trading lets you invest ______________________________

  ____

B. Entertainment and media [p. 10.15]

Entertainment and media-related Web sites can take many forms, such as music, videos, news, sporting events, and 3-D multiplayer games. Streaming allows users to access and use a file while it is transmitting, thus supporting live videos and concerts. MP3 music files can be purchased and downloaded to a hard disk.

C. Travel [p. 10.15]

Travel-related Web sites can provide directions or do cost-comparison work. A shopping bot is ______________________________

____

D. Health [p. 10.16]

Health-related Web sites can maintain databases of doctors and dentists and provide chat rooms for patients. At pharmacy sites, you can refill prescriptions or ask pharmacists questions.

E. Other business services [p. 10.17]

Other areas of service include ______________________________

____

VI. Creating an online store [p. 10.17]

Regardless of the scope or size of business, all e-commerce must address some common concerns.

A. Building an electronic storefront [p. 10.18]

Some e-retailers develop and maintain their Web site in house, while others outsource all or part of the system.

- E-commerce software allows ______________________________
  ____
- A Web host is ______________________________
  ____

Companies that outsource part of their site usually outsource the transaction services that require a secure server. A secure server is ______________

____

B. Managing payments [p. 10.20]

Credit cards are the most popular payment method on the Web.

To accept credit cards safely, a business must:

(1) ______________________________

(2) ______________________________

(3) ______________________________

A merchant account establishes ______________________________

____

An order form is used to collect customer orders and credit card information.

Payment-processing software manages the transaction between the e-retailer and the bank.

Electronic money (e-money) is ______________________________

____

C. Fulfillment [p. 10.22]

Fulfillment includes managing and storing inventory, packaging and shipping products, and maintaining records of transactions.

A fulfillment service can provide ______________________________

____

D. Attracting and retaining customers [p. 10.22]

A successful Web site attracts customers and keeps them returning to the site.

eCRM (electronic Customer Relationship Management) combines __________

____

- The customer life cycle begins ______________________________
  ____
- Collaborative browsing is ______________________________
  ____

E-mail publishing is ______________________________

____

E. Web site management [p. 10.24]

By monitoring Web site use, e-retailers can collect data and use it to improve their Web sites.

F. Promoting the Web site [p. 10.24]

Choosing a name for the Web site and an associated domain name can be a crucial decision. Domain names influence the number of hits a Web page receives. A domain name should be registered with search engines to ensure that the Web site will appear in hit lists for searches on related keywords. A submission service is ______________________________

____

Sites can be promoted with banner ads, which are ______________________________

____

A click-through occurs ______________________________

____

Another form of promotion, called spam, usually generates antagonism instead of sales. Spam is ______________________________

____

Self Test

Matching

1. ____ B2C e-commerce
2. ____ C2C e-commerce
3. ____ online auction
4. ____ P2P
5. ____ B2B e-commerce
6. ____ vendor B2B site
7. ____ service B2B site
8. ____ brokering B2B site
9. ____ informediary B2B site
10. ____ B2E e-commerce

a. similar to negotiating, in which one consumer puts goods up for sale to other consumers
b. consists of the sale and exchange of products and services between businesses
c. acts as a middleman by negotiating the contract of a purchase and a sale
d. consists of the sale of products or services from a business to the general public
e. an Internet network that enables users to connect hard disks and exchange files directly
f. uses a network to provide one or more services to businesses
g. use of intranet technology to handle activities within a business
h. consists of individuals using the Internet to sell directly to other individuals
i. product supplier that allows purchasing agents to use a network to shop and submit RFQs
j. allows users to pay bills directly from their computers
k. searches the Internet for the best price on a product or service
l. provides specialized information about suppliers and other businesses

True/False

____ 1. The last step in the development of e-commerce was electronic data interchange, created to increase paperwork and decrease response time.

____ 2. The least popular vehicle for C2C (consumer-to-consumer) e-commerce is the online auction.

____ 3. A revenue stream is the method a business uses to generate income.

____ 4. Few users take advantage of online storage services for the purpose of storing backup copies of data and information.

____ 5. After the bank approves a transaction, the e-retailer processes the order and sends it to the fulfillment center where it is packaged and shipped.

____ 6. Few investors prefer online stock trading because the transaction fee for each trade usually is substantially more than when trading through a broker.

____ 7. Some health-related Web sites maintain databases of doctors and dentists to help you find the one that suits your needs.

____ 8. Although using e-commerce software requires a very small financial outlay, it gives the merchant little control over its e-retail site.

____ 9. An e-retail site developer must realize that all merchandise transfers equally well to the Web.

____ 10. Surveys indicate that a large percentage of customers are dissatisfied with customer services at online businesses.

Multiple Choice

____ 1. What term sometimes is used to identify e-commerce that takes place using mobile devices?
   a. t-commerce
   b. m-commerce
   c. d-commerce
   d. h-commerce

____ 2. What is the set of standards that control the transfer of business data and information among computers both within and among companies?
   a. electronic software distribution (ESD)
   b. automated transfer manipulation (ATM)
   c. electronic data interchange (EDI)
   d. online revenue stream (ORS)

____ 3. Instead of shipping their products, what do some businesses use to sell products such as software, music, movies, books, and photographs?
   a. electronic software distribution (ESD)
   b. automated transfer manipulation (ATM)
   c. electronic data interchange (EDI)
   d. online revenue stream (ORS)

____ 4. What Microsoft Web applications enable users to access Microsoft software on the Web from any type of device that can connect to the Internet?
   a. .MIC
   b. .WEB
   c. .APP
   d. .NET

____ 5. In e-retail, what is a shopping cart?
   a. a software component that allows a merchant to set up a storefront
   b. a Web site where an e-retailer displays it products
   c. a Web site that searches for the best price on a product or service
   d. a software component that allows customers to collect purchases

____ 6. What allows you to pay bills from your computer; that is, transfer money electronically from your account to a payee's account?
   a. online banking
   b. online shopping
   c. online trading
   d. online retailing

____ 7. What does a secure server do?
   a. establishes a relationship between a bank and e-retail users
   b. delivers Web pages to interested users
   c. prevents access to a system by unauthorized users
   d. provides data storage to computer users

____ 8. What can provide warehousing and inventory management, product assembly, order processing, packing, shipping, return processing, and online reporting?
   a. logistic companies
   b. vertical companies
   c. digital companies
   d. informediary companies

____ 9. What is the process of sending newsletters via e-mail messages to a large group of people with similar interests?
   a. e-mail broadcasting
   b. e-mail circulating
   c. e-mail distributing
   d. e-mail publishing

____ 10. When does a click-through occur?
   a. when a visitor clicks an item to transfer it to a shopping cart
   b. when a visitor clicks an ad to move to the advertiser's Web page
   c. when a visitor clicks an order form to enter financial information
   d. when a visitor clicks a submission service to register with search engines

Fill in the Blanks

1. ____________________ is a financial business transaction that occurs over an electronic network.
2. With ____________________, B2C businesses sell directly to consumers without using traditional retail channels.
3. A(n) ____________________ is the interrelated network of facilities and distribution methods that obtains materials, transforms materials into finished products, and delivers the finished products to customers.
4. Sometimes called ____________________ e-commerce, this type of B2B e-commerce site specializes in a particular industry.
5. A(n) ____________________ is a computer that delivers Web pages to users.
6. A(n) ____________________ is the Web site where an e-retailer displays its products.
7. A(n) ____________________ is a Web site that searches the Internet for the best price on a product or service in which you are interested.
8. ____________________ allows a merchant to set up a storefront with a product database, combined with a shopping cart.
9. A(n) ____________________ is a Web server in e-commerce environments.

10. The ____________________ establishes a relationship between an e-retailer and a bank, which allows the e-retailer to accept credit card payments.

Complete the Table

FACTORS THAT LEAD TO E-LOYALTY

• ____________________
• ____________________
• ____________________
• Easy of use/navigation
• ____________________
• ____________________
• ____________________
• Quality of storefront/product representation
• ____________________
• ____________________
• Quality of customer support

Things to Think About

1. What advantages do clicks-and-mortar businesses have over bricks-and-mortar businesses? Are there any disadvantages to being a clicks-and-mortar business?
2. How could more than one e-commerce revenue stream be used at a single Web site?
3. What are the advantages of shopping at an electronic storefront when compared with shopping at a traditional store? What are the disadvantages?
4. When providing for e-commerce, what concerns (building a storefront, managing payment, managing product delivery, designing a site that attracts and keeps customers, managing the site, and promoting the site) are most important? What decisions are least important? Why?

Puzzle

Use the given clues to complete the crossword puzzle.

E-Commerce

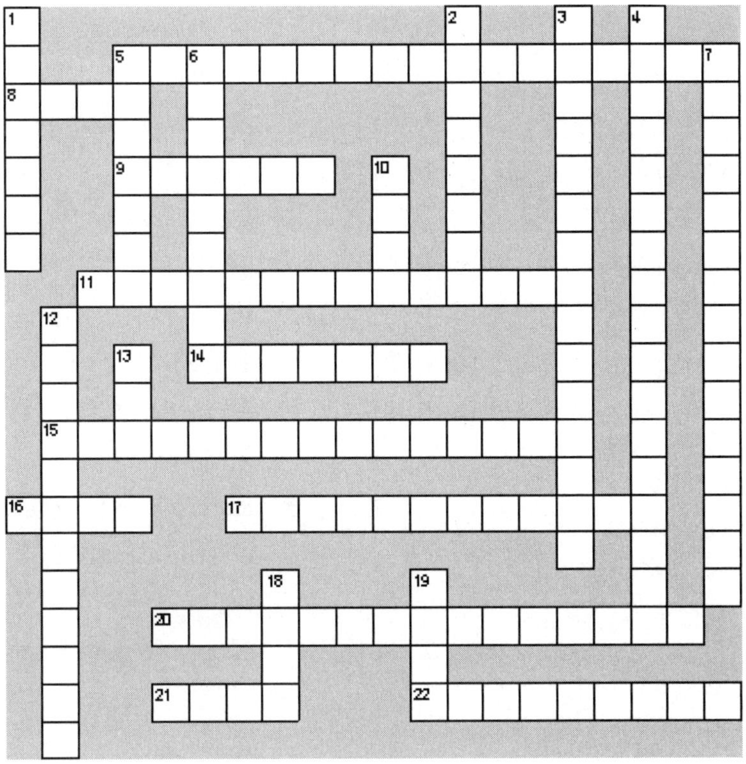

Across

5. Web-based business that registers a domain name with hundreds of search engines
8. E-commerce that refers to the use of intranet technology to handle activities within a business
9. Type of B2B site that is a product supplier
11. Software application that exists on a Web site
14. Web site that searches the Internet for the best price on a product or service
15. Company that has a bricks-and-mortar location as well as an online presence
16. E-commerce that consists of the sale of products or services to the general public
17. Software component that allows customers to collect e-retail purchases
20. Establishes a relationship between an e-retailer and a bank
21. Unsolicited e-mail messages or newsgroup postings
22. Type of B2B site that acts as a middleman by negotiating the contract of a purchase

Down

1. Outside company that provides the hardware, software, and communications required for a Web server
2. Internal network that uses Internet technologies
3. Company that has a physical location
4. Maximizing benefits by eliminating the middleman
5. Type of B2B site that provides one or more services
6. Online advertisement that displays a brief message
7. Process of sending newsletters via e-mail to a large group of people
10. E-commerce that consists of individuals selling products and services directly to other individuals
12. Occurs when a visitor clicks an advertisement to move to the sponsor's Web page
13. Set of standards that control the transfer of business data and information
18. E-commerce strategy that combines personalized touch and customized service
19. E-commerce that consists of the sale and exchange of products and service between businesses

Self Test Answers

Matching

1. *d* [p. 10.04]
2. *h* [p. 10.06]
3. *a* [p. 10.06]
4. *e* [p. 10.06]
5. *b* [p. 10.06]
6. *i* [p. 10.07]
7. *f* [p. 10.07]
8. *c* [p. 10.07]
9. *l* [p. 10.07]
10. *g* [p. 10.08]

True/False

1. *F* [p. 10.04]
2. *F* [p. 10.06]
3. *T* [p. 10.08]
4. *F* [p. 10.11]
5. *T* [p. 10.13]
6. *F* [p. 10.14]
7. *T* [p. 10.16]
8. *F* [p. 10.18]
9. *F* [p. 10.20]
10. *T* [p. 10.23]

Multiple Choice

1. *b* [p. 10.03]
2. *c* [p. 10.04]
3. *a* [p. 10.08]
4. *d* [p. 10.08]
5. *d* [p. 10.12]
6. *a* [p. 10.14]
7. *c* [p. 10.20]
8. *a* [p. 10.22]
9. *d* [p. 10.24]
10. *b* [p. 10.25]

Fill in the Blanks

1. *Electronic commerce (e-commerce)* or *E-business* [p. 10.02]
2. *disintermediation* [p. 10.04]
3. *supply chain* [p. 10.07]
4. *vertical B2B* [p. 10.08]
5. *Web server* [p. 10.10]
6. *electronic storefront* or *online catalog* [p. 10.12]
7. *shopping bot* or *shopbot* [p. 10.15]
8. *E-commerce software* [p. 10.18]
9. *e-commerce server* or *commerce server* [p. 10.19]
10. *merchant account* [p. 10.20]

Complete the Table

FACTORS THAT LEAD TO E-LOYALTY

- *Price*
- *Selection*
- *Web site appearance*
- Easy of use/navigation
- *Availability of information*

- *Ease of ordering*
- *Posted privacy policies*
- Quality of storefront/product representation
- *Shipping*
- *On-time delivery*
- Quality of customer support

Things to Think About

Answers will vary.

Puzzle Answer

E-Commerce

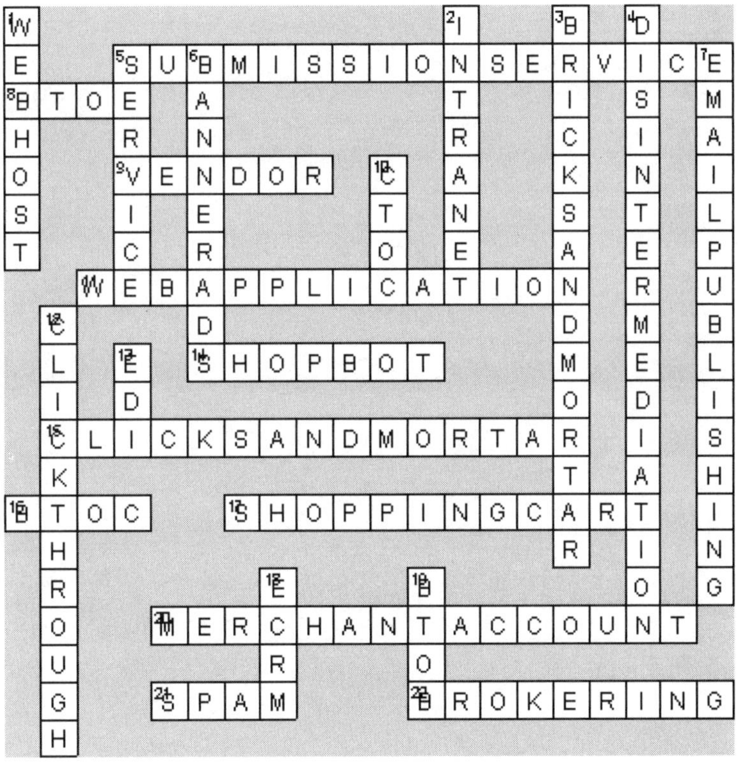

NOTES

DISCOVERING COMPUTERS 2003

STUDY GUIDE

CHAPTER 11

Computers and Society: Home, Work, and Ethical Issues

Chapter Overview

This chapter presents ways in which the computer has changed society. You learn how computers are used at home and in many fields such as education, entertainment, finance, government, health care, science, publishing, and travel. You discover how emerging technologies are being used in everyday life. Health issues and preventions related to computers also are presented. Finally, the chapter discusses ethical issues surrounding computer use.

Chapter Objectives

After completing this chapter, you should be able to:

- Understand that computers have made a tremendous difference in daily living
- Explain how computers are used at home
- Describe how computers change the way society interacts with disciplines such as education, entertainment, finance, government, health care, science, publishing, and travel
- Recognize the issues associated with the digital divide
- Understand how e-commerce affects the way people conduct business
- Identify ways virtual reality, intelligent agents, and robots are being used in daily life
- Learn how to prevent health-related disorders and injuries due to computer use
- Understand how to design a workspace ergonomically
- Recognize symptoms of computer addiction
- Explain green computing
- Understand ethical issues surrounding computer use

Chapter Outline

I. Living with computers [p. 11.02]

Computers have changed almost every aspect of society. Although society has benefited greatly from computers, the use of computers has raised some important issues.

A. At home [p. 11.03]

The main reason computers have infiltrated the home is because people want access to the Web. Home users connect to the Web to:

- ______________________________
- ______________________________
- ______________________________
- ______________________________
- ______________________________
- ______________________________
- ______________________________
- ______________________________

Internet appliances are ______________________________

____

B. Education [p. 11.06]

Education is ______________________________

____

Computer-based training (CBT) helps ______________________________

____

Web-based training (WBT) is ______________________________

____

Advantages of CBT and WBT over traditional training:

- ______________________________
- ______________________________
- ______________________________

  Simulations are ______________________________
- ______________________________

WBT, CBT, and other materials are combined for distance learning courses.

Distance learning (DL) is ______________________________

____

Another form of CBT is edutainment. Edutainment is ______________________________

____

C. Digital divide [p. 11.09]

The digital divide is the idea that you can separate people of the world into two distinct groups:

(1) ______________________________

(2) ______________________________

A number of programs have been begun to narrow the digital divide.

- The Anytime Anywhere Learning (AAL) program provides ______________________________

  ____

- PowerUp is ______________________________

____

D. Entertainment [p. 11.11]

A computer provides hours of entertainment. In addition to playing exciting games, you can view fine art, listen to music, watch or compose a video, or edit photographs. These forms of entertainment are available on CD-ROM, DVD-ROM, and on the Web.

A digital camera allows ______________________________

____

E. E-commerce [p. 11.13]

Electronic commerce is ______________________________

____

One of the most popular uses of e-commerce is shopping. Users purchase items through an electronic storefront or an online auction.

- An electronic storefront contains ______________________________

  ____

  A shopping cart allows ______________________________
- With an online auction you bid ______________________________

  ____

F. Finance [p. 11.14]

Some people use personal finance software to balance ______________________________

____

- With online banking, you transfer ______________________________

  ____
- With online stock trading, you can ______________________________

  ____

G. Government [p. 11.16]

Most U.S. government offices have Web sites to provide citizens with up-to-date information. Employees of government agencies also use computers as part of their routines. Some companies provide government services on the Web, allowing the public to complete transactions, such as filing taxes or applying for permits and licenses, online.

H. Health care [p. 11.18]

Nearly every aspect of the medical field uses computers:

- Hospitals and doctors maintain ______________________________

  ____

- Computers monitor ______________________________
____
- Doctors using ______________________________
____
- Pharmacists use ______________________________
____
- Computers and computerized devices assist ______________________________
____
- Doctors use e-mail to communicate ______________________________
____
- Surgeons implant ______________________________
____
- Surgeons use ______________________________
____

Telemedicine affords ______________________________
____

Computer-aided surgery (CAS) involves ______________________________
____

I. Science [p. 11.21]

All branches of science use computers to assists with collecting, analyzing, and modeling data. Scientists also use the Internet to communicate with colleagues. Much of the success related to computers in the medical field is a result of breakthroughs made by scientists.

Today's voice recognition software is a result of experimentation using neural networks. A neural network is ______________________________
____

J. Publishing [p. 11.22]

Publishing is ______________________________
____

Many publishers make the content of magazines and newspapers available online.

An electronic book (e-book) is ______________________________
____

K. Travel [p. 11.24]

A GPS (global positioning system) reports ______________________________
____

Onboard navigation systems offer many worthwhile features:

- ______________________
- ______________________
- ______________________
- ______________________
- ______________________
- ______________________
- ______________________
- ______________________
- ______________________

People can use the Web to shop for a car, to obtain travel directions, or to reserve a car, hotel, or flight. Many vehicles and airplanes also provide other computer-related options.

L. Telecommuting [p. 11.26]

Telecommuting is ____

____

Workers telecommute to:

1. ____
2. ____
3. ____
4. ____

II. Emerging technologies [p. 11.27]

Technologies once considered *high tech* are emerging in everyday applications.

A. Virtual reality [p. 11.27]

Virtual reality (VR) is ____

____

A VR world is ____

Virtual reality has many practical applications: ______________________

____

____

B. Intelligent agents [p. 11.28]

Artificial intelligence (AI) is ____

____

- An intelligent agent is ____

  ____

  IntelliSense™ technology corrects ______________________________

  ____

- A network agent is ____

  ____

C. Robots [p. 11.30]

A robot is ______________________________

____

As the cost drops, more homes will be using robots.

- AIBO the robot dog has ______________________________
- CareBot is ______________________________

III. A healthy work environment [p. 11.30]

The widespread use of computers has led to some important health concerns.

A. Computers and health risks [p. 11.30]

Repetitive stress injury (RSI) is ______________________________

____

Computer-related RSIs include tendonitis and carpal tunnel syndrome.

- Tendonitis is ______________________________

  ____

- Carpal tunnel syndrome (CTS) is ______________________________

  ____

Another health-related condition due to computer usage is computer vision syndrome (CVS). You may have CVS if you have: ______________________________

____

B. Ergonomics and workplace design [p. 11.32]

Ergonomics is ______________________________

____

Characteristics of a well-designed work area: ______________________________

____

____

____

The MPR II standard defines ______________________________

C. Computer addiction [p. 11.32]

Computer addiction occurs ______________________________

____

Symptoms of computer addiction:

- ______________________________
- ______________________________
- ______________________________
- ______________________________
- ______________________________
- ______________________________

D. Green computing [p. 11.33]

Green computing involves ____

____

The ENERGY STAR program encourages ___________________________

____

IV. Ethics and society [p. 11.34]

Computer ethics are ____

____

Often discussed areas of computer ethics are information accuracy, intellectual property rights, and codes of conduct.

A. Information accuracy [p. 11.34]

Many people access information maintained by other people or companies, such as on the Internet. You should evaluate the value of a Web page before relying on its content. Concerns also arise about the ethics of using computers to alter output, such as retouching photographs.

B. Intellectual property rights [p. 11.36]

Intellectual property (IP) rights are ______________________________

____

IP issues include copyright and trademark infringement.

- A copyright gives ____

  ____

  Software piracy is _______________________________________

  Copyright law gives the public fair use to copyrighted material, which allows use for educational and critical purposes.

- A trademark protects _____________________________________

  ____

  The controversy with trademarks relates __________________________

  ____

C. Codes of conduct [p. 11.37]

An IT (information technology) code of conduct is ____________________

____

____

Self Test

Matching

1. ____ Internet appliance
2. ____ simulations
3. ____ edutainment
4. ____ digital camera
5. ____ electronic storefront
6. ____ online auction
7. ____ telemedicine
8. ____ neural network
9. ____ virtual reality (VR)
10. ____ robot

a. allows you to take pictures and store the photographic images digitally
b. ideal for the family that uses the computer only for Web access
c. system that attempts to simulate the behavior of the human brain
d. use of computers to simulate an environment that appears as three-dimensional space
e. computer-based models of real-life situations used to learn skills in hazardous situations
f. contains descriptions, graphics, and a shopping cart
g. affords access to medical care through computers with videoconferencing capabilities
h. sophisticated type of intelligent agent that performs tasks on remote computers
i. type of educational software that combines education with entertainment
j. computer-controlled device that can move and react to feedback from the outside world
k. allows money to be transferred electronically from your account to a payee's account
l. allows visitors to bid on an item, with the highest bidder purchasing the item

True/False

____ 1. Home computers are available in only one color and design.

____ 2. The cost of personal computers has increased, so few schools or businesses can afford to equip labs or classrooms with computers.

____ 3. Few national or international companies offer DL (distance learning) training.

____ 4. Society is attempting to make technology accessible to everyone, including those with disabilities.

____ 5. Anyone with access to a computer, an Internet connection, and a means to pay for purchased goods or services can participate in e-commerce.

____ 6. With Web-based online banking, all of your account information is stored on your own personal computer.

____ 7. Employees that telecommute tend to have lower job satisfaction and are less productive.

____ 8. AI (artificial intelligence) technology can sense your actions and, based on logical assumptions and prior experience, take an appropriate action to complete a task.

____ 9. To help prevent back injury when working at a computer, take a break every 30 to 60 minutes — stand up, walk around, or stretch.

____ 10. A copyright protects any tangible form of expression.

Multiple Choice

____ 1. Why do home users connect to the Web?
   a. to shop for goods and services
   b. to bank and invest
   c. to communicate with others
   d. all of the above

____ 2. What is a type of CBT that uses Internet technology?
   a. Web-based training (WBT)
   b. computer-aided instruction (CAI)
   c. resource system instruction (RSI)
   d. Internet activity development (IAD)

____ 3. In the digital divide, what group is considered part of the *have-nots*?
   a. upper income families
   b. minority neighborhoods
   c. educated people
   d. people without disabilities

____ 4. What is e-commerce?
   a. a financial business transaction that occurs over an electronic network
   b. the process of developing markets through instruction
   c. using computer simulations to assist in learning shopping techniques
   d. a work arrangement in which employees work away from the workplace

____ 5. For what can you *not* use personal finance software?
   a. balance a checkbook
   b. track personal income and expenses
   c. write letters to creditors
   d. evaluate financial plans

____ 6. Prior to performing surgery on live humans, what do many surgeons use?
   a. CVS
   b. CTS
   c. CAS
   d. CAI

____ 7. How do *employers* benefit when employees telecommute?
   a. reduced time and expense spent traveling
   b. reduction in overhead
   c. flexible work schedule
   d. comfortable work environment

____ 8. AIBO and CareBot are examples of what emerging technology?
   a. intelligent agents
   b. simulations
   c. virtual reality
   d. robots

____ 9. Sore, tired, burning, itching, or dry eyes are symptoms of what condition?
   a. CTS
   b. CVS
   c. CBT
   d. CAI

____ 10. In an ergonomic workplace, what should be the viewing angle to the center of the screen?
   a. 20°
   b. 40°
   c. 60°
   d. 90°

Fill in the Blanks

1. A(n) ____________________ allows an e-commerce buyer to collect purchases.
2. ____________________ is a short range wireless communications technology that can be used to obtain airline tickets, event tickets, train tickets, and coupons.
3. ____________________ involves using computer simulations to assist in learning surgical techniques.
4. A(n) ____________________ is an entire 3-D Web site, containing infinite space and depth, that is created using special VR software.
5. AI experts promoted the advantages of ____________________, or software with built-in intelligence.
6. A network agent, sometimes called a(n) ____________________, can be used to search the Web or other networks for information.
7. A(n) ____________________ is an injury or disorder of the muscles, nerves, tendons, ligaments, and joints.
8. ____________________ is an affliction attributed to users addicted to the Internet.
9. ____________________ refers to work created by inventors, authors, and artists.
10. ____________________ is the unauthorized and illegal duplication of copyrighted software.

Complete the Table

PREVENTING COMPUTER-RELATED HEALTH RISKS

HAND EXERCISES
• Spread ______________________________
• Gently push ______________________________
• Dangle ______________________________
TECHNIQUES TO EASE EYESTRAIN
• Every 10 to 15 minutes, take an eye break.
– Look ______________________________
– Roll ______________________________
– Close ______________________________
• Blink ______________________________
• Place ______________________________
• Use ______________________________
• Use ______________________________
• If you wear glasses, ask ______________________________
• Adjust ______________________________

Things to Think About

1. Why are Internet appliances ideal for the family that uses the computer only for Web access? When might a family want a personal computer instead of an Internet appliance?
2. What subjects, and what age levels, are best suited to CBT (computer-based training) and WBT (Web-based training)? Why? What subjects, or what age levels, are better suited to traditional training? Why?
3. In terms of the digital divide, what gap that separates the *haves* from the *have-nots* (see Figure 11-13 on page 11.10) would be easiest to bridge? What gap would be hardest to close? Why?
4. Is it ethical to post any of the following on the Web? Why or why not?
   - material authored by someone else
   - scanned photos or pages from a book
   - song lyrics by a recording artist
   - your own or someone else's term paper

Puzzle

All of the words described below appear in the puzzle. Words may be either forward or backward, across, up and down, or diagonal. Circle each word as you find it.

Computers and Society

```
                                      K D S C
                                      S Z E C
                                      N T C I
                                        B N
                                        T A
                            M U U B N E N I
              R A T S Y G R E N E O L E O L
O X G N I D A R T K C O T S E N I L N O R P
I N T E L L I G E N T A G E N T E O U S F P
K R O W T E N L A R U E N K C C B A I I E A
V S V I R T U A L R E A L I T Y V W R M R T
V H C C O D E O F C O N D U C T Y S Q U O E
D O B L U E T O O T H D A C I A B M C L T N
T P S V P E R S O N A L F I N A N C E A S R
H P U R E W O P S R P K R A M E D A R T C E
G I Y S C I H T E R E T U P M O C E S I I T
I N G R O B O T O N L I N E A U C T I O N N
R G G N I T U P M O C N E E R G K A T N O I
Y C A R I P E R A W T F O S T R A M S S R D
P A L V M R A R E M A C L A T I G I D T T L
O R F O T E N D O N I T I S               C R
C T C Y P N L                             E O
                                          L W
                                          E R
                                          L V
```

Ideal for those who only want Web access

Helps students learn by using computers and instructional software

Type of CBT that uses Internet technology

Computer-based models of real life

Delivery of education at one location while the learning takes place at another

Nationwide industry partnership whose goal is to place technology in schools

Stores photographed images digitally instead of on film

Contains descriptions, graphics, and a shopping cart

Allows e-commerce buyers to collect purchases

Web site where bids are made on an item

Short range wireless communications technology

Type of software used to balance a checkbook

Allows stocks to be bought and sold without using a broker

Uses computer simulations to assist in learning surgical techniques

Simulates the behavior of the human brain

Reports a car's location via satellites

Simulates an environment that appears as 3-D space

3-D site that contains infinite space and depth

Application of human intelligence to computers

Software with built-in intelligence

Program that asks questions and carries out tasks on behalf of a user

Searches the Web or other networks for information

Computer-controlled device that can move and react to feedback

Injury of the muscles, nerves, tendons, ligaments, and joints

Inflammation of a tendon due to repeated motion or stress

Inflammation of the nerve that connects the forearm to the palm

Eye condition due to computer usage

Occurs when the computer consumes someone's entire social life

Condition of users addicted to the Internet

Reduces electricity and environmental waste while using a computer

Government program that promotes energy-efficient devices

Moral guidelines that govern computer use

Work created by inventors, authors, and artists

Gives exclusive rights to duplicate, publish, and sell material

Illegal duplication of copyrighted software

Protects a company's logos and brand names

Written guideline that helps determine whether a computer action is ethical

Self Test Answers

Matching

1. *b* [p. 11.05]
2. *e* [p. 11.07]
3. *i* [p. 11.08]
4. *a* [p. 11.12]
5. *f* [p. 11.14]
6. *l* [p. 11.14]
7. *g* [p. 11.19]
8. *c* [p. 11.22]
9. *d* [p. 11.27]
10. *j* [p. 11.30]

True/False

1. *F* [p. 11.04]
2. *F* [p. 11.06]
3. *F* [p. 11.08]
4. *T* [p. 11.10]
5. *T* [p. 11.13]
6. *F* [p. 11.15]
7. *F* [p. 11.26]
8. *T* [p. 11.28]
9. *T* [p. 11.31]
10. *T* [p. 11.36]

Multiple Choice

1. *d* [p. 11.04]
2. *a* [p. 11.06]
3. *b* [p. 11.11]
4. *a* [p. 11.13]
5. *c* [p. 11.14]
6. *c* [p. 11.20]
7. *b* [p. 11.26]
8. *d* [p. 11.30]
9. *b* [p. 11.31]
10. *a* [p. 11.32]

Fill in the Blanks

1. *shopping cart* [p. 11.14]
2. *Bluetooth™* [p. 11.14]
3. *Computer-aided surgery (CAS)* [p. 11.20]
4. *VR world* [p. 11.27]
5. *smart software* [p. 11.28]
6. *bot* [p. 11.29]
7. *musculoskeletal disorder (MSD)* or *repetitive stress injury (RSI)* [p. 11.30]
8. *Internet addiction disorder (IAD)* [p. 11.32]
9. *Intellectual property (IP)* [p. 11.36]
10. *Software piracy* [p. 11.36]

Complete the Table

PREVENTING COMPUTER-RELATED HEALTH RISKS

HAND EXERCISES
• Spread *fingers apart for several seconds while keeping wrists straight.*
• Gently push *back fingers and then thumb.*
• Dangle *arms loosely at sides and then shake arms and hands.*
TECHNIQUES TO EASE EYESTRAIN
• Every 10 to 15 minutes, take an eye break.
– Look *into the distance and focus on an object for 20 to 30 seconds.*
– Roll *your eyes in a complete circle.*
– Close *your eyes and rest them for at least a minute.*
• Blink *your eyes every five seconds.*
• Place *your display device an arm's length from your eyes with the top of the screen at eye level.*
• Use *a glare screen.*
• Use *large fonts.*
• If you wear glasses, ask *your doctor for computer glasses.*
• Adjust *the lighting.*

Things to Think About

Answers will vary.

Puzzle Answer

Computers and Society

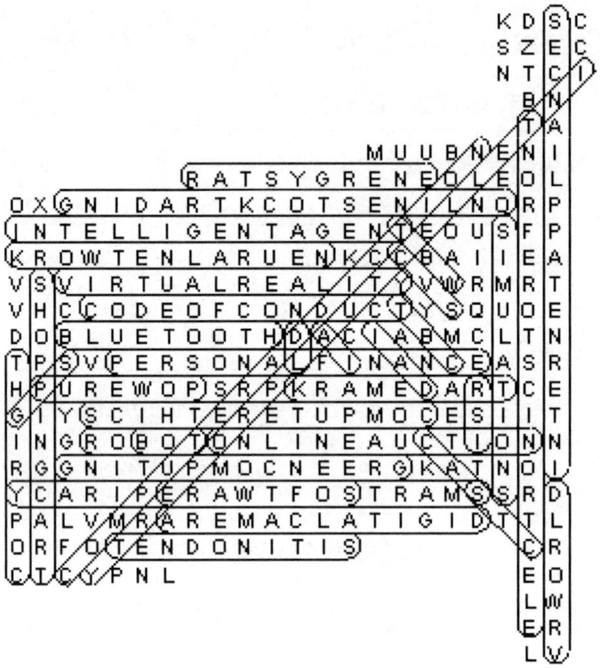

DISCOVERING COMPUTERS 2003

STUDY GUIDE

CHAPTER 12

Computers and Society: Security and Privacy

Chapter Overview

This chapter identifies some potential risks to computers and software. You discover the safeguards that schools, businesses, and individuals can implement to minimize these risks. Internet security risks and safeguards also are discussed. Finally, the chapter presents actions you can take to keep your personal information private.

Chapter Objectives

After completing this chapter, you should be able to:

- Identify the various types of security risks that can threaten computers
- Recognize how a computer virus works and take the necessary steps to prevent viruses
- Describe ways to safeguard a computer
- Understand how to create a good password
- Identify various biometric devices
- Recognize that software piracy is illegal
- Explain why encryption is necessary
- Determine why computer backup is important and how it is accomplished
- Discuss the steps in a disaster recovery plan
- Understand ways to secure an Internet transaction
- List ways to protect your personal information

Chapter Outline

I. Computer security: risks and safeguards [p. 12.02]

A computer security risk is ____

____

A computer crime is ____

____

Safeguards are ____

A. Computer viruses [p. 12.02]

A computer virus is ______________________________

____

Viruses are activated in three basic ways:

(1) ______________________________

(2) ______________________________

(3) ______________________________

Most computers become infected with viruses through an e-mail attachment. Before opening or executing any e-mail attachment, you should ensure that the e-mail message is from a trusted source. A trusted source is ___________

____

Main types of viruses:

- A boot sector virus executes ______________________________

  ____

- A file virus attaches ______________________________

  ____

- A macro virus uses ______________________________

  ____

Many viruses activate as soon as an infected file is accessed or run.

Some viruses activate based on specific criterion:

- A logic bomb is ______________________________
- A time bomb is ______________________________

A malicious-logic program (malware) is ______________________________

____

Viruses are a type of malware. Other types of malware:

- A worm is ______________________________

  ____

  Code Red was ______________________________
- A Trojan horse is ______________________________

  ____

B. Virus detection and removal [p. 12.05]

An antivirus program protects ______________________________

____

Antivirus programs can detect viruses by looking for virus signatures or by inoculating existing program files.

- A virus signature is ____

  ____

  A polymorphic virus modifies ______________________________

  ____

- To inoculate a program file, the antivirus program records ____________

  ____

  A stealth virus infects ______________________________________

  ____

If a virus cannot be removed, the infected file can be quarantined or, for boot sector viruses, the computer can be restarted with a recovery disk.

- A quarantine is ____

  ____

- A recovery disk is ____

  ____

A virus hoax is ____

C. Unauthorized access and use [p. 12.07]

Unauthorized access is ____

____

- A hacker, or cracker, is ____

  ____

Unauthorized use is ____

____

Access controls can prevent unauthorized access and use.

An access control is ____

____

Access controls often are implemented using a two-phase process:

- Identification verifies ____

  ____

- Authentication verifies ____

  ____

Methods of identification and authorization:

1. User names and passwords [p. 12.08]

   A user name is ____

   ____

   A password is ____

   ____

2. Possessed objects [p. 12.10]
   A possessed object is ____

   ____

   - A personal identification number (PIN) is __________________________

     ____

3. Biometric devices [p. 12.10]
   A biometric device authenticates ____________________________________

   ____

   Types of biometric devices:
   - A fingerprint scanner captures _____________________________________

     ____
   - A hand geometry system measures ___________________________________

     ____
   - A face recognition system captures _________________________________

     ____
   - A voice recognition system compares ________________________________

     ____
   - A signature verification system recognizes ___________________________

     ____
   - An iris recognition system reads____________________________________

     ____

4. Callback system [p. 12.12]
   With a callback system, you can _____________________________________

   ____

   - An audit trail records ____

     ____

D. Hardware theft [p. 12.13]
   Hardware theft is ____

   ____

   Hardware vandalism is ____

   ____

   To reduce the chances of hardware theft, companies and individuals can ____

   ____

   ____

   ____

E. Software theft [p. 12.14]

Software theft can be physically stealing the media containing the software, but the most common form of software theft is software piracy.

Software piracy is ____

____

A license agreement is ____

A single-user license agreement permits users to:

- ____
- ____
- ____

  ____

A single-user license agreement does not permit users to:

- ____
- ____
- ____
- ____

During product activation, users provide ______________________________

____

The Business Software Alliance (BSA) operates __________________________

____

To reduce costs, companies can obtain a site license or network site license.

- A site license gives ____

  ____
- A network site license allows ____________________________________

  ____

F. Information theft [p. 12.15]

Information theft occurs ____

____

1. Encryption [p. 12.16]

   Encryption is ____

   ____

   - Plaintext is ____
   - Ciphertext is ____
   - An encryption key is _____________________________________

     ____

Basic types of encryption:

- Private key encryption uses ______________________________
  ____
  - The data encryption standard (DES) is ____________________
    ____
- Public key encryption uses ______________________________
  ____
  - RSA encryption is ______________________________
    ____
  - Fortezza is ______________________________
    ____

G. System failure [p. 12.18]

A system failure is ______________________________

____

Electrical disturbances:

- Noise is ______________________________
- An undervoltage occurs ______________________________
  ____
  A brownout is ______________________________
  A blackout is ______________________________
- An overvoltage occurs ______________________________
  ____
  A spike occurs ______________________________

A surge protector uses ______________________________

____

Surge protectors should meet specifications of the Underwriters Laboratories (UL) 1449 standard and have a Joule (the unit of energy that can be absorbed before damage occurs) rating of at least 200.

An uninterruptible power supply (UPS) is ______________________________

____

- A standby UPS switches ______________________________
- An online UPS always runs ______________________________

H. Backup procedures [p. 12.19]

A backup is ______________________________

____

To back up a file, you make ______________________________

To restore a file, you copy ______________________________

Types of backup:

- A full backup copies ______________________________

  ____
- A differential backup copies ______________________________

  ____
- An incremental backup copies ______________________________

  ____

Backup procedures specify ______________________________

____

A three-generation backup policy preserves ______________________________

____

- The grandparent is ______________________________
- The parent is ______________________________
- The child is ______________________________

An online backup service is ______________________________

____

I. Disaster recovery plan [p. 12.21]

A disaster recovery plan is ______________________________

____

Disaster recovery plan components:

1. The emergency plan [p. 12.21]

   An emergency plan specifies ______________________________

   ____
2. The backup plan [p. 12.21]

   The backup plan specifies ______________________________

   ____
3. The recovery plan [p. 12.21]

   The recovery plan specifies ______________________________

   ____
4. The test plan [p. 12.21]

   The test plan contains ______________________________

   ____

J. Developing a computer security plan [p. 12.22]

A computer security plan summarizes ______________________

____

A computer security plan should:

1. ______________________
2. ______________________
3. ______________________

II. Internet and network security [p. 12.22]

Information transmitted over networks has a higher degree of security risk.

A. Denial of service attacks [p. 12.22]

A denial of service attack (DoS attack) occurs ______________________

____

A DDoS (distributed DoS) attack is ______________________

____

A zombie is ______________________

The Computer Emergency Response Team Coordination Center (CERT®/CC) is ______________________

B. Securing Internet transactions [p. 12.23]

A secure site is ______________________

Secure sites use digital certificates along with a security protocol, such as SSL or S-HTTP, and sometimes the SET specification.

1. Digital certificates [p. 12.23]

A digital certificate is ______________________

____

2. Secure Sockets Layer [p. 12.24]

Secure Sockets Layer (SSL) provides ______________________

____

3. Secure HTTP [p. 12.24]

Secure HTTP (S-HTTP) allows ______________________

____

4. Secure Electronic Transaction [p. 12.24]

The Secure Electronic Transaction (SET) specification uses ______________________

____

C. Securing e-mail messages [p. 12.24]

When you send e-mail over the Internet, just about anyone can read it. Two ways to protect an e-mail message are to encrypt it and to sign it digitally.

- Pretty Good Privacy (PCP) is ________________________________
  ____
- A digital signature is ________________________________
  ____

D. Firewalls [p. 12.24]

A firewall is ________________________________

____

A proxy server is ________________________________

____

A personal firewall is ________________________________

____

An online security service is ________________________________

____

III. Information privacy [p. 12.26]

Information privacy refers ________________________________

____

Companies and employers use several techniques to collect personal data.

A. Electronic profiles [p. 12.27]

Electronic profiles can include very personal data. National marketing firms and Internet advertising firms create electronic profiles of individuals by combining merchant databases with information from public sources.

B. Cookies [p. 12.28]

A cookie is ________________________________

____

Web sites use cookies for a variety of purposes:

- ________________________________
- ________________________________
- ________________________________
- ________________________________
- ________________________________

C. Spyware [p. 12.30]

Spyware is ______________________________

____

- Adware is ______________________________
- A Web bug is ______________________________

D. Spam [p. 12.31]

Spam is ______________________________

____

- E-mail filtering is ______________________________
- An anti-spam program attempts ______________________________

E. Privacy laws [12.32]

Common points in federal and state laws regarding the storage and disclosure of personal data:

1. ______________________________
2. ______________________________
3. ______________________________
4. ______________________________

Federal laws dealing specifically with computers:

- Electronic Communications Privacy Act (ECPA) provides ______________________________

  ____
- Computer Matching and Privacy Protection Act regulates ______________________________

  ____
- Computer Fraud and Abuse Acts outlaw ______________________________

  ____
- Fair Credit Reporting Act limits ______________________________

  ____

F. Employee monitoring [p. 12.33]

Employee monitoring involves ______________________________

____

The proposed Privacy for Consumers and Workers Act states ______________________________

____

G. Protecting children from objectionable material [p. 12.34]

Web filtering software is ______________________________

____

Self Test

Matching

1. ____ boot sector virus
2. ____ file virus
3. ____ macro virus
4. ____ logic bomb
5. ____ time bomb
6. ____ worm
7. ____ Trojan horse
8. ____ antivirus program
9. ____ polymorphic virus
10. ____ stealth virus

a. identifies and removes any viruses in memory, on a storage media, or on incoming files
b. infects a program file, but still reports the size and creation date of the uninfected program
c. duplicates all of the program and data files in the computer
d. copies itself repeatedly in memory or on a disk drive until no memory or disk space remains
e. executes when a computer boots up because it resides in the boot sector
f. converts readable data into unreadable characters to prevent unauthorized access
g. uses the macro language of an application to hide virus code
h. activates on a particular date
i. modifies its program code each time it attaches itself to another program or file
j. attaches itself to program files
k. activates when it detects a certain condition
l. hides within or looks like a legitimate program

True/False

____ 1. The increased use of networks, the Internet, and e-mail has accelerated the spread of computer viruses because users easily can share infected files.

____ 2. Completely effective methods exist to ensure that a computer or network is safe from computer viruses and other malware.

____ 3. Biometric devices grant access using computer analysis of a biometric identifier, which is a mental or emotional characteristic.

____ 4. Site license fees usually cost significantly less than purchasing individual copies of software for each computer at a single location.

____ 5. The lower the Joule rating of a surge protector, the better the protection.

____ 6. Generally, users should perform a differential or incremental backup at regular intervals, and a full backup between each differential or incremental backup.

____ 7. In developing a computer security plan, keep in mind that some degree of risk is unavoidable.

____ 8. Web pages that use SSL typically begin with the http, instead of https.

____ 9. An unprotected e-mail sent through the Internet is similar to sending a postcard through the United States mail.

____ 10. Online shopping sites generally use a session cookie to keep track of items in your shopping cart.

Multiple Choice

____ 1. What type of virus often is hidden in templates so it will infect any document using the template?
   a. boot sector virus
   b. file virus
   c. system virus
   d. macro virus

____ 2. Which of the following is *not* a tip you should use when selecting a password?
   a. use a combination of letters, digits, words, initials, and dates
   b. use a password you can type without looking at the keyboard
   c. use your name or the name of a family member
   d. use something that no one but you would know

____ 3. Why are biometric devices gaining popularity as a security precaution?
   a. they are a virtually foolproof method of identification
   b. they are unaffected by physical conditions or feelings of stress
   c. they cannot transmit germs
   d. all of the above

____ 4. What does a single-user license agreement typically permit a user to do?
   a. install the software on a network
   b. make one copy for backup
   c. give copies to friends and colleagues
   d. rent or lease the software

____ 5. Why is software piracy a serious offense?
   a. it increases the chance of viruses
   b. it reduces your ability to receive technical support
   c. it drives up the price of software for all users
   d. all of the above

____ 6. What type of backup provides the best protection against data loss but can be time consuming?
   a. full backup
   b. partial backup
   c. differential backup
   d. incremental backup

____ 7. In a three-generation backup, what are the oldest copy, second oldest copy, and most recent copy of the file called?
   a. child, parent, grandparent
   b. grandparent, parent, child
   c. child, grandparent, parent
   d. parent, grandparent, child

____ 8. What disaster recovery plan component should contain names and telephone numbers of people and organizations to be notified, procedures to follow with equipment, evacuation procedures, and return procedures?
   a. the emergency plan
   b. the backup plan
   c. the recovery plan
   d. the test plan

____ 9. Which of the following is *not* a common point in laws regarding the storage and disclosure of personal data?
   a. information collected and stored should be limited to what is necessary to carry out the function of the collecting business or government agency
   b. once collected, access should be restricted to employees within the organization who need access to it to perform their jobs
   c. personal information can be released outside the organization collecting the data regardless of whether or not the person has agreed to its release
   d. an individual should know the data is being collected and have the opportunity to determine the accuracy of the data

____ 10. What law did the Supreme Court declare unconstitutional in 1997 because it violated the guarantee of free speech?
   a. the Electronic Communications Privacy Act
   b. the Communications Decency Act
   c. the Computer Matching and Privacy Protection Act
   d. the Computer Fraud and Abuse Act

Fill in the Blanks

1. The term ____________________ refers to online or Internet-based illegal acts.
2. The programmer of a virus, known as a(n) ____________________, intentionally writes a virus program.
3. An early government proposal used an encryption formula in a tamper-resistant personal computer processor called the ____________________.
4. The government's ____________________ plan proposed using independent escrow organizations that would have custody of private keys that could decode encrypted messages.
5. Backup copies should be kept ____________________, which means in a location separate from the computer site.

6. A firm may enter into a(n) ____________________ with another firm, where one firm provides space and sometimes equipment to the other in case of a disaster.

7. Companies and individuals who need help with computer security plans can contact the ____________________ via telephone or on the Web for assistance.

8. A(n) ____________________ is an authorized company or person that issues and verifies digital certificates.

9. A(n) ____________________ is a mathematical formula that generates a code from the contents of an e-mail message.

10. To collect information about user's Web browsing habits, some Internet advertising firms use spyware, which in this case is called ____________________.

Complete the Table

MAJOR U.S. GOVERNMENT LAWS CONCERNING PRIVACY

DATE	LAW	PURPOSE
1998	____________________ ____________________	Makes it illegal to circumvent anti-piracy schemes in commercial software.
1998	Child Online Protection Act (COPA)	____________________ ____________________
1997	____________________ ____________________	Closed a loophole in the law that allowed people to give away copyrighted material on the Internet.
_____	National Information Infrastructure Protection Act	Penalizes theft of information across state lines, threats against networks, and computer system trespassing.
1994	Computer Abuse Amendments Act	____________________ ____________________
1988	____________________ ____________________	Regulates the use of government data to determine the eligibility of individuals for federal benefits.
_____	Electronic Communications Privacy Act (ECPA)	Provides the protection that covers mail and telephone communications to electronic communications.
1984	Computer Fraud and Abuse Act	____________________ ____________________
1974	____________________ ____________________	Forbids federal agencies from allowing information to be used for a reason other than for which it was collected.

Things to Think About

1. Four methods of identification and authentication are user names and passwords, possessed objects, biometric devices, and callback systems. What are the advantages of each method? What are the disadvantages?
2. In response to the problem of information theft, two government proposals were Clipper chip and the key escrow plan. How are the proposals different? Why do you think each proposal has been opposed?
3. The goal of a computer security plan is to match an appropriate level of safeguards against the identified risks. What is meant by this? How might this goal affect the security plans of an individual, a school, a business, and a government agency?
4. Laws regarding information privacy, employee monitoring, and protecting children from objectionable material on the Internet remain incomplete. For which area is the need for legislation most pressing? Why?

Puzzle

Use the given clues to complete the crossword puzzle.

Security and Privacy

Across

1. Unauthorized and illegal duplication of copyrighted programs
4. Provides help with computer security plans via telephone or the Web
7. In a three-generation backup plan, the most recent copy of the file
9. Authenticates a person by verifying personal characteristics
10. Most popular private key encryption system
13. File that records both successful and unsuccessful access attempts
16. Series of characters that matches an entry in an authorization file
19. Program that copies itself repeatedly into memory
21. Powerful public key encryption technology
22. Verifies an individual is who he or she claims to be
23. Amount of energy a surge protector can absorb before it is damaged
24. Type of backup that duplicates only files that have changed since the last full backup
26. Numeric password
27. Protective measures taken to minimize security risks

Down

1. Momentary overvoltage
2. Item that must be carried to gain access to a computer or computer facility
3. Type of virus that activates on a particular date
5. Unwanted electrical signal mixed with normal voltage entering the computer
6. Known pattern of virus code
8. Verifies an individual is a valid user
11. Common type of license included with software purchased by individual users
12. Type of virus that replaces the program used to start the computer
14. Formed by a number of software companies to combat piracy
15. Potentially damaging program designed to negatively affect the way a computer works
17. In a three-generation backup plan, the oldest copy of the file
18. Individual who accesses a computer or network illegally
20. Disk that contains an uninfected copy of key operating system commands
25. Uses batteries to provide electricity for a limited amount of time

Self Test Answers

Matching

1. *e* [p. 12.04]
2. *j* [p. 12.04]
3. *g* [p. 12.04]
4. *k* [p. 12.04]
5. *h* [p. 12.04]
6. *d* [p. 12.04]
7. *l* [p. 12.04]
8. *a* [p. 12.05]
9. *i* [p. 12.06]
10. *b* [p. 12.06]

True/False

1. *T* [p. 12.02]
2. *F* [p. 12.05]
3. *F* [p. 12.10]
4. *T* [p. 12.15]
5. *F* [p. 12.19]
6. *F* [p. 12.20]
7. *T* [p. 12.22]
8. *F* [p. 12.24]
9. *T* [p. 12.24]
10. *T* [p. 12.29]

Multiple Choice

1. *d* [p. 12.04]
2. *c* [p. 12.09]
3. *a* [p. 12.12]
4. *b* [p. 12.14]
5. *d* [p. 12.15]
6. *a* [p. 12.20]
7. *b* [p. 12.21]
8. *a* [p. 12.21]
9. *c* [p. 12.32]
10. *b* [p. 12.34]

Fill in the Blanks

1. *cybercrime* [p. 12.02]
2. *virus author* [p. 12.02]
3. *Clipper chip* [p. 12.17]
4. *key escrow* [p. 12.17]
5. *offsite* [p. 12.19]
6. *reciprocal backup relationship* [p. 12.21]
7. *International Computer Society Association (ICSA)* [p. 12.22]
8. *certificate authority* or *issuing authority* [p. 12.23]
9. *hash* [p. 12.24]
10. *adware* [p. 12.31]

Complete the Table

MAJOR U.S. GOVERNMENT LAWS CONCERNING PRIVACY

DATE	LAW	PURPOSE
1998	*Digital Millennium Copyright Act (DCMA)*	Makes it illegal to circumvent anti-piracy schemes in commercial software.
1998	Child Online Protection Act (COPA)	*Penalizes online commercial entities that knowingly distribute material deemed harmful to minors.*
1997	*No Electronic Theft (NET) Act*	Closed a loophole in the law that allowed people to give away copyrighted material on the Internet.
1996	National Information Infrastructure Protection Act	Penalizes theft of information across state lines, threats against networks, and computer system trespassing.
1994	Computer Abuse Amendments Act	*Amends 1984 act to outlaw transmission of harmful computer code such as viruses.*
1988	*Computer Matching and Privacy Protection Act*	Regulates the use of government data to determine the eligibility of individuals for federal benefits.

DATE	LAW	PURPOSE
1986	Electronic Communications Privacy Act (ECPA)	Provides the protection that covers mail and telephone communications to electronic communications.
1984	Computer Fraud and Abuse Act	*Outlaws unauthorized access to government computers.*
1974	*Privacy Act*	Forbids federal agencies from allowing information to be used for a reason other than for which it was collected.

Things to Think About

Answers will vary.

Puzzle Answer

Security and Privacy

DISCOVERING COMPUTERS 2003

STUDY GUIDE

CHAPTER 13

Databases and Information Management

Chapter Overview

This chapter reviews data and information concepts and presents methods for maintaining high-quality data. The advantages of organizing data in a database are discussed and various types of databases are described. You learn about the role of the database analysts and administrators. Finally, the chapter outlines the qualities of valuable information and presents various types of information systems.

Chapter Objectives

After completing this chapter, you should be able to:

- Explain why data and information are important to an organization
- Identify file maintenance techniques
- Differentiate between the file processing and database approaches
- Discuss the advantages of using a database management system (DBMS)
- Describe characteristics of relational and object-oriented databases
- Explain how to use a query language
- Understand how Web databases work
- Discuss the responsibilities of the database analysts and administrators
- Identify the qualities of valuable information
- Describe the various types of information systems
- Understand the concept of a data warehouse

Chapter Outline

I. Data and information [p. 13.02]

- Data is ____
- Information is ____

Computers process data into information.

A database is ____

____

A. Data integrity [p. 13.03]

Data integrity is____

Garbage in, garbage out (GIGO) is a computer phrase that means ____________

____

II. The hierarchy of data [p. 13.04]

Data is organized in a hierarchy in which each higher level consists of one or more elements from the lower level preceding it.

- A character — such as a letter, number, punctuation mark, or other symbol — is represented by a byte (8 bits grouped together in a unit).
- A field is ____
  A field name uniquely identifies each field.
  Characteristics such as data type and field size define each field.
  The data type specifies ____________________________________
  Common data types include:
  - ____________ • ____________ • ____________
  - ____________ • ____________ • ____________
  - ____________ • ____________
  The field size defines ____________________________________
- A record is ____
  A key field is ____
- A data file is ____
  ____
  Program files are _______________________________________
  ____
- A database includes a group of related data files.

III. Maintaining data [p. 13.06]

File maintenance refers ____________________________________

A. Adding records [p. 13.06]

Records are added when ____________________________________

B. Changing records [p. 13.06]

Generally, you change records for two reasons:

(1) ____

(2) ____

C. Deleting records [p. 13.08]

A record is deleted from a file when ___________________________

D. Data validation [p. 13.09]

Validation is ____

Validation rules reduce ______________________________

Types of validity checks:

1. Alphabetic/numeric check [p. 13.09]

   An alphabetic check ensures ______________________________

   ____

   A numeric check ensures ______________________________

2. Range check [p. 13.09]

   A range check determines ______________________________

   ____

3. Consistency check [p. 13.09]

   A consistency check tests ______________________________

   ____

4. Completeness check [p. 13.10]

   A completeness check verifies ______________________________

   ____

5. Check digit [p. 13.10]

   A check digit confirms ______________________________

   ____

IV. File processing versus databases [p. 13.11]

A. File processing systems [p. 13.11]

In a typical file processing system, each department has ______________

____

____

Disadvantages of file processing systems:

- Data redundancy — ______________________________

  ____

- Isolated data — ______________________________

  ____

B. The database approach [p. 13.12]

With the database approach, many programs and users can ______________

____

Users can access the data in a database using database software, also called a database management system (DBMS). Instead of working with a DBMS, some users interact with a front end.

A front end is ______________________________

A back end is ______________________________

Advantages of the database approach:

- Reduced data redundancy — ______________________________
- Improved data integrity — ______________________________
- Shared data — ______________________________
- Reduced development time — ______________________________
- Easier reporting — ______________________________

Disadvantages of the database approach: ______________________________

V. Database management systems [p. 13.14]

A database management system (DBMS) is ______________________________

Common elements of a DBMS:

A. Data dictionary [p. 13.14]

A data dictionary contains ______________________________

A DBMS uses the data dictionary to perform validation checks and maintain the integrity of data. The data dictionary allows a default value to be specified. A default value is ______________________________

B. File maintenance and retrieval [p. 13.15]

A query is ______________________________

A DBMS offers several methods to access its data.

1. Query language [p. 13.16]

A query language consists ______________________________

2. Query by example [p. 13.17]
   Query by example (QBE) has ______________________________

   ____

3. Form [p. 13.17]
   A form is ____

   ____

   An electronic form (e-form) typically uses ________________

   ____

4. Report generator [p. 13.18]
   A report generator allows ______________________________

   ____

C. Data security [p. 13.19]
   Access privileges define ________________________________

   ____

   - With read-only privileges, you can ____________________

     ____

   - With full-update privileges, you can __________________

     ____

D. Backup and recovery [p. 13.20]
   A DBMS provides a variety of techniques to restore a database:
   - A backup is ____
   - A log is ____
     The before image is ____________________________________
     The after image is _____________________________________
   - A DBMS often provides a recovery utility to restore a database.
     In a rollforward, the DBMS uses ________________________

     ____

     In a rollback, the DBMS uses __________________________

     ____

VI. Relational, object-oriented, and multidimensional databases [p. 13.21]
   A data model consists __________________________________

   ____

   Three popular data models are relational, object-oriented, and multidimensional.
   Object-relational databases combine ______________________

   ____

A. Relational databases [p. 13.22]

A relational database stores ______________________________

____

Data Terminology		
File Processing Developer	Relational Database Developer	Relational Database User
File	______________	______________
Record	______________	______________
Field	______________	______________

A relationship is ______________________________

____

Normalization is ______________________________

____

1. Relational algebra [p. 13.24]

   Relational algebra uses ______________________________

   ____

   Relational operations:

   - The projection operation retrieves ______________________________

     ____

   - The selection operation retrieves ______________________________

     ____

   - The join operation combines ______________________________

     ____

2. Structured Query Language [p. 13.25]

   Structured Query Language (SQL) is ______________________________

   ____

B. Object-oriented databases [p. 13.26]

An object-oriented database (OODB) stores ______________________________

An object is ______________________________

____

Advantages of an object-oriented database relative to relational databases:

____

____

____

Applications appropriate for an object-oriented database:

- ____________________
- ____________________
- ____________________
- ____________________
- ____________________

1. Object query language [p. 13.27]
   An object query language (OQL) is ____________________

   ____

C. Multidimensional databases [p. 13.27]
   A multidimensional database (MDDB) stores ____________________

   ____

   The key advantage of the multidimensional database is ____________________

   ____

   ____

VII. Web databases [p. 13.28]

Much of the information on the Web exists in databases. Users access and provide information to Web databases by entering data into a form on a Web page, the front end to the database.

A database server is ____________________

____

A CGI (Common Gateway Interface) script manages ____________________

____

VIII. Database administration [p. 13.30]

The role of coordinating the use of a database belongs to the database analysts and administrators, who need cooperation from all database users.

A. Role of the database analysts and administrators [p. 13.30]
   The data analyst (DA) focuses ____________________

   ____

   The database administrator (DBA) creates ____________________

   ____

B. Role of the employee as a user [p. 13.30]
   The user's responsibilities are ____________________

   ____

C. Database design guidelines [p. 13.30]

These guidelines make it easier for a user to query a database:

1. Determine ____________________
2. Design ____________________
   ____
3. Design ____________________
   ____
   ____
4. Determine ____________________

IX. Qualities of valuable information [p. 13.30]

Valuable information is accurate, verifiable, timely, organized, useful, accessible, and cost-effective.

- Accurate information is ____________________
- Verifiable means ____________________
- Timely information has ____________________
- Organized information is ____________________
- Useful information has ____________________
- Accessible information is ____________________
- Cost-effective information costs ____________________

A. How managers use information [p. 13.32]

Managers are ____________________

____

Management activities:

- Planning involves ____________________
  ____
- Organizing includes ____________________
  ____
- Leading involves ____________________
  ____
- Controlling involves ____________________
  ____

B. Levels of users [p. 13.32]

Typically, the information users in an organization are classified into four levels: executive management, middle management, operational management, nonmanagement employees.

1. Executive management [p. 13.32]
   Executive management includes ______________________________
   ____
   Strategic decisions focus ______________________________
   ____
2. Middle management [p. 13.33]
   Middle management is ______________________________
   ____
   Tactical decisions apply ______________________________
   ____
3. Operational management [p. 13.33]
   Operational management supervises ______________________________
   ____
   An operational decision involves ______________________________
   ____
4. Nonmanagement employees [p. 13.33]
   Nonmanagement employees ______________________________
   ____
   Empowering is ______________________________
   ____

X. Types of information systems [p. 13.34]
An information system is ______________________________
____
A procedure is ______________________________
Categories of information systems:
A. Office information systems [p. 13.34]
   An office information system (OIS) is ______________________________
   ____
   All levels of users benefit from an OIS.
B. Transaction processing systems [p. 13.35]
   A transaction processing system (TPS) is ______________________________
   ____
   - With batch processing, the computer collects ______________________________
     ____

- With online transaction processing (OLTP), the computer processes _____

____

Today, most transaction processing systems use OLTP.

C. Management information systems [p. 13.36]

A management information system (MIS) is ______________________________

____

An MIS generates three types of information:

- A detailed report lists ______________________________
- A summary report consolidates ______________________________
- An exception report identifies ______________________________

____

D. Decision support systems [p. 13.37]

A decision support system (DSS) helps ______________________________

____

A DSS uses data from internal and external sources.

- Internal sources might include ______________________________

____

- External sources could include ______________________________

____

An executive information system (EIS) is ______________________________

____

E. Data warehouses [p. 13.38]

A data warehouse is ______________________________

____

Web farming is ______________________________

____

A click stream is ______________________________

____

A distributed database exists in______________________________

A data mart contains ______________________________

Data mining is ______________________________

F. Expert systems [p. 13.40]

An expert system is ______________________________

____

Expert systems are composed of a knowledge base and inference rules.

- A knowledge base is ____

  ____

- Inference rules are ____

  ____

Artificial intelligence (AI) is ____

____

G. Integrated information systems [p. 13.41]

____

____

____

Self Test

Matching

1. ____ executive management
2. ____ middle management
3. ____ operational management
4. ____ nonmanagement employees
5. ____ office information system
6. ____ transaction processing system
7. ____ management information system
8. ____ decision support system
9. ____ executive information system
10. ____ expert system

a. a special type of DSS designed to support the information needs of senior management
b. responsible for tactical decisions that apply specific programs and plans
c. captures and stores the knowledge of human authorities and then imitates human reasoning and decision-making
d. production, clerical, and staff personnel who frequently need information to do their jobs
e. captures and processes data from day-to-day business activities
f. stockholders and observers responsible for investment decisions
g. generates accurate, timely, and organized information for managerial activities
h. increases productivity and assists with communications among employees
i. responsible for strategic decisions that focus on overall goals and objectives
j. designed to help users reach a determination when an uncertain situation arises
k. make operational decisions that involve a company's day-to-day activities
l. implemented to identify errors in hardware, software, data, or procedures

True/False

____ 1. In the hierarchy of data, a field contains records, a record contains files, and a file contains databases.

____ 2. Deleting unneeded records reduces the size of files and creates additional storage space.

____ 3. Two of the advantages of file processing systems are no data redundancy and shared data.

____ 4. Database management systems are available for many sizes and types of computers.

____ 5. Like a form, you use report generators to retrieve and maintain data.

____ 6. In a rollback, or backward recovery, the DBMS uses the log to re-enter changes made to the database since the last database save or backup.

____ 7. A database typically is based on multiple data models.

____ 8. Hypermedia databases contain text, graphics, video, and sound.

____ 9. Most information finds its value with time.

____ 10. Expert systems help all levels of users make decisions.

Multiple Choice

____ 1. What is the smallest unit of data that you can access?
   a. a character
   b. a field
   c. a record
   d. a file

____ 2. What does a completeness check do?
   a. ensures that only the correct type of data is entered into a field
   b. tests data in multiple fields to determine if a relationship is reasonable
   c. determines whether a number is within a specified range
   d. verifies a required field contains data

____ 3. Which of the following is *not* an advantage of the database approach?
   a. reduced data redundancy
   b. decreased vulnerability
   c. improved data integrity
   d. easier reporting

____ 4. A report generator, or report writer, is used only for what purpose?
   a. to enter data
   b. to change data
   c. to retrieve data
   d. to maintain data

____ 5. Access, Informix, Paradox, and Visual FoxPro are popular DBMSs based on what data model?
   a. relational databases
   b. object-oriented databases
   c. object-relational databases
   d. multidimensional databases

____ 6. How does a relational database developer refer to a record?
   a. as a table
   b. as a relation
   c. as a tuple
   d. as an attribute

____ 7. In relational algebra, what operation retrieves data from columns (fields)?
   a. the projection operation
   b. the selection operation
   c. the consistency operation
   d. the join operation

____ 8. When designing the fields for each database table, what should you *not* do?
   a. be sure every field has a unique primary key
   b. use separate fields for logically distinct items
   c. set default values for frequently entered data
   d. create fields for information that can be derived from other entries

____ 9. Activities such as recording a business activity, confirming an action or causing a response, and maintaining data are associated with what category of information systems?
   a. office information systems (OIS)
   b. transaction processing systems (TPS)
   c. management information systems (MIS)
   d. decision support systems (DSS)

____ 10. What type of report consolidates data so you can review it quickly and easily?
   a. a detail report
   b. a projection report
   c. a summary report
   d. an exception report

Fill in the Blanks

1. A(n) ____________________ includes a collection of data organized so you can access, retrieve, and use the data.
2. ____________________ are types of executable files that may or may not use data files.
3. ____________________ minimize data entry errors and enhance the integrity of data before a program writes the data on disk.
4. A(n) ____________________ is software that allows you to create, access, and manage a database.
5. Some call the data dictionary ____________________ because it contains data about data.
6. A(n) ____________________ is a window on the screen that provides areas for entering or changing data in a database.
7. In addition to data, a relational database stores data ____________________, which are connections within the data.
8. A relational database is a two-dimensional table, but a(n) ____________________ can store more than two dimensions of data.
9. Many people initially referred to the functions of a TPS (transaction processing system) as ____________________.
10. ____________________ is the application of human intelligence to computers.

Complete the Table

POPULAR DATABASE MANAGEMENT SYSTEMS

Database	Manufacturer	Computer Type
Access	____________	Handheld and desktop computers, server
Approach	Lotus Development Corporation	____________
____________	IBM Corporation	Personal computer, server, mid-range server, mainframe
GemStone	____________	Server, mid-range server
____________	Oracle Corporation	Handheld and desktop computers, server, mid-range server, mainframe
Paradox®	____________	Personal computer, server
SQL Server™	Microsoft Corporation	____________
____________	Microsoft Corporation	Personal computer, server

Things to Think About

1. Why are deleted records sometimes *flagged* so they are not processed, instead of being removed immediately?
2. What type of validity check — alphabetic/numeric, range, consistency, completeness, or check digit — would be most useful when reviewing your answers on an exam? Why?
3. What characteristics of valuable information are most important? On what, if any, factors might your answer depend? Why?
4. What categories of information systems (OIS, TPS, MIS, DSS, and expert systems) would each level in an organization (executive management, middle management, operational management, and nonmanagement) be most likely to use? Why?

Puzzle

Use the given clues to complete the crossword puzzle.

Databases and Information Management

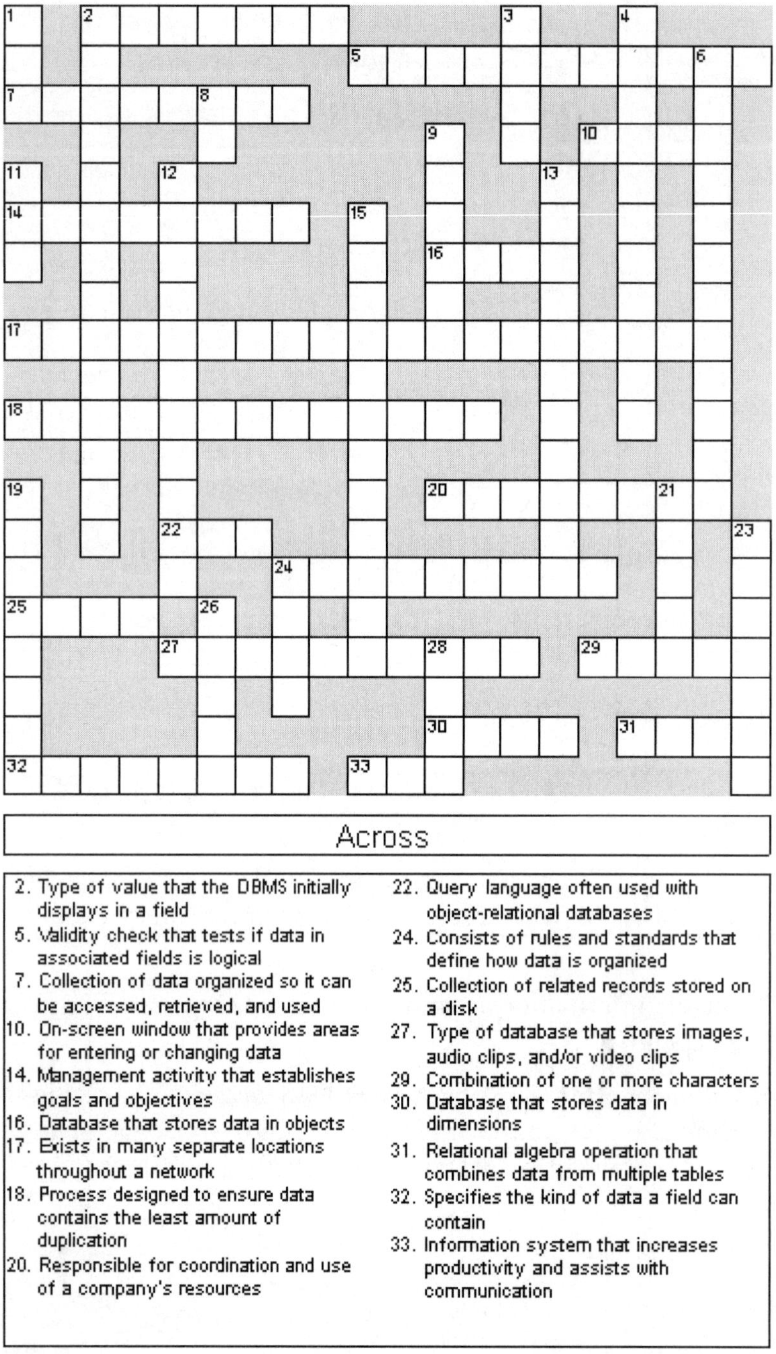

Across

2. Type of value that the DBMS initially displays in a field
5. Validity check that tests if data in associated fields is logical
7. Collection of data organized so it can be accessed, retrieved, and used
10. On-screen window that provides areas for entering or changing data
14. Management activity that establishes goals and objectives
16. Database that stores data in objects
17. Exists in many separate locations throughout a network
18. Process designed to ensure data contains the least amount of duplication
20. Responsible for coordination and use of a company's resources
22. Query language often used with object-relational databases
24. Consists of rules and standards that define how data is organized
25. Collection of related records stored on a disk
27. Type of database that stores images, audio clips, and/or video clips
29. Combination of one or more characters
30. Database that stores data in dimensions
31. Relational algebra operation that combines data from multiple tables
32. Specifies the kind of data a field can contain
33. Information system that increases productivity and assists with communication

Down

1. Type of database that stores data about engineering and scientific designs
2. Computer that stores and provides access to a Web database
3. Acronym for "Garbage in, garbage out"
4. Copy of a record prior to a change
6. Validity check that verifies a required field contains data
8. Application of human intelligence to computers
9. Group of related fields
11. Information system that captures and processes data from day-to-day activities
12. Data that is organized, meaningful, and useful
13. Links to an e-form on a Web page
15. Imitates human reasoning and decision making
19. Uniquely identifies each record in a file
21. Validity check that determines whether a number is within specified limits
23. Management activity that instructs and authorizes others to perform tasks
24. Collection of raw unprocessed facts, figures, and symbols
26. Request for specific data from a database
28. Software that allows a database to be created, accessed, and managed

Self Test Answers

Matching

1. *i* [p. 13.32]
2. *b* [p. 13.33]
3. *k* [p. 13.33]
4. *d* [p. 13.33]
5. *h* [p. 13.34]
6. *e* [p. 13.35]
7. *g* [p. 13.36]
8. *j* [p. 13.37]
9. *a* [p. 13.38]
10. *c* [p. 13.40]

True/False

1. *F* [p. 13.04]
2. *T* [p. 13.08]
3. *F* [p. 13.11]
4. *T* [p. 13.14]
5. *F* [p. 13.19]
6. *F* [p. 13.20]
7. *F* [p. 13.21]
8. *T* [p. 13.26]
9. *F* [p. 13.30]
10. *T* [p. 13.40]

Multiple Choice

1. *b* [p. 13.04]
2. *d* [p. 13.10]
3. *b* [p. 13.13]
4. *c* [p. 13.19]
5. *a* [p. 13.19]
6. *c* [p. 13.22]
7. *a* [p. 13.24]
8. *d* [p. 13.31]
9. *b* [p. 13.35]
10. *c* [p. 13.36]

Fill in the Blanks

1. *database* [p. 13.02]
2. *Program files* [p. 13.05]
3. *Validity checks* or *Validation rules* [p. 13.09]
4. *database management system (DBMS)* [p. 13.14]
5. *metadata* [p. 13.15]
6. *form* or *data entry form* [p. 13.17]
7. *relationships* [p. 13.22]
8. *multidimensional database (MDDB)* [p. 13.27]
9. *data processing* [p. 13.35]
10. *Artificial intelligence (AI)* [p. 13.41]

Complete the Table

POPULAR DATABASE MANAGEMENT SYSTEMS

Database	Manufacturer	Computer Type
Access	*Microsoft Corporation*	Handheld and desktop computers, server
Approach	Lotus Development Corporation	*Personal computer, server*
DB2	IBM Corporation	Personal computer, server, mid-range server, mainframe
GemStone	*GemStone Systems, Inc.*	Server, mid-range server

Database	Manufacturer	Computer Type
*Oracle*________	Oracle Corporation	Handheld and desktop computers, server, mid-range server, mainframe
Paradox®	*Corel Corporation*________	Personal computer, server
SQL Server™	Microsoft Corporation	*Server*________________
*Visual FoxPro*___	Microsoft Corporation	Personal computer, server

Things to Think About

Answers will vary.

Puzzle Answer

Databases and Information Management

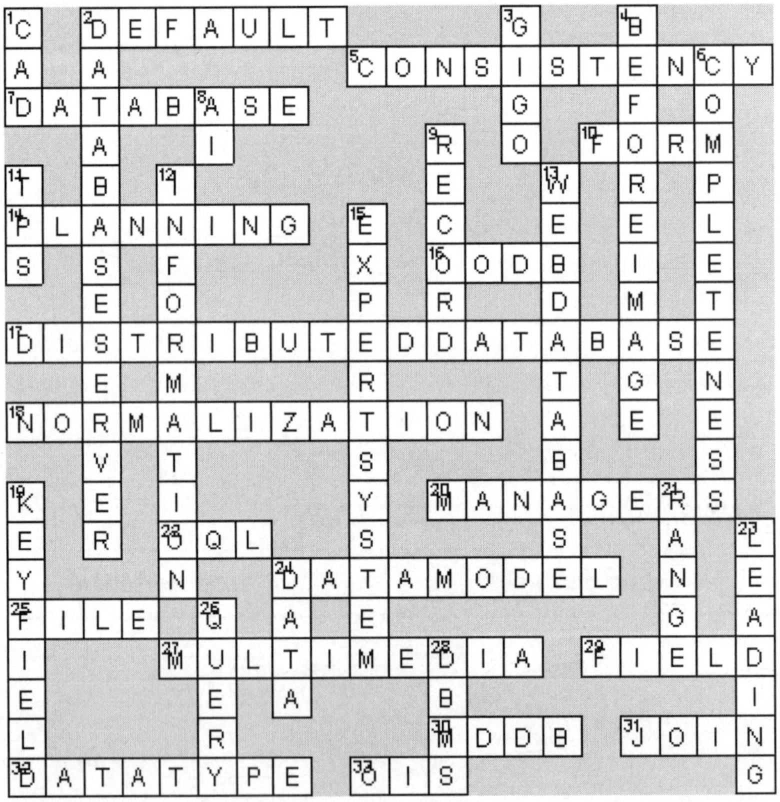

DISCOVERING COMPUTERS 2003

STUDY GUIDE

CHAPTER 14

Information System Development

Chapter Overview

This chapter discusses the phases in the system development life cycle. The guidelines for system development also are presented. The chapter introduces activities that occur during the entire SDLC such as project management, feasibility assessment, data and information gathering, and documentation. Throughout the chapter, a case study about a fictitious company called Web Lane Café illustrates and reinforces activities performed during each phase of the life cycle.

Chapter Objectives

After completing this chapter, you should be able to:

- Explain the phases in the system development life cycle
- Identify the guidelines for system development
- Recognize the responsibilities of various IT professionals
- Discuss the importance of project management, feasibility assessment, data and information gathering techniques, and documentation
- Describe how structured tools such as entity-relationship diagrams and data flow diagrams are used in analysis and design
- Differentiate between packaged software and custom software
- Identify program development as part of the system development life cycle
- Discuss techniques used to convert to a new system
- Understand how IT professionals support an information system

Chapter Outline

I. What is the system development life cycle? [p. 14.02]

A system is ____

____

An information system is ____

____

The system development life cycle (SDLC) is ______________________________

____

Some IT professionals refer to the entire system development process as software engineering.

A. Phases in the SDLC [p. 14.02]

The system development life cycle can be grouped into these phases:

1. ________________ 3. ________________ 5. ________________

2. ________________ 4. ________________

The phases form a loop; that is, information system development is an ongoing process.

B. Guidelines for system development [p. 14.03]

Information system development should follow three guidelines:

(1) ____

(2) ____

Users include ______________________________________

(3) ____

Standards are ______________________________________

C. Who participates in the system development life cycle? [p. 14.04]

A systems analyst is ______________________________________

____

The steering committee is ______________________________________

A project team is ______________________________________

The project leader manages ______________________________________

D. Project management [p. 14.05]

Project management is ______________________________________

____

The project leader identifies:

- ____
- ____
- ____
- ____
- ____
- ____

The project leader usually records these items in a project plan.

- A Gantt chart is ______________________________________

  ____

- A deliverable is ______________________________________

  ____

Project leaders can use project management software to ______________________

____

E. Feasibility assessment [p. 14.06]

Feasibility is ____

____

Criteria used to test project feasibility:

- Operational feasibility measures ______________________________

  ____

- Schedule feasibility measures ______________________________

  ____

- Technical feasibility measures ______________________________

  ____

- Economic feasibility measures ______________________________

  ____

F. Documentation [p. 14.07]

Documentation is ____

____

A project notebook contains ______________________________________

Well-written, ongoing, thorough documentation makes it easier to work with and modify existing systems.

G. Data and information gathering techniques [p. 14.07]

Techniques used during the SDLC to gather data and information:

- ____
- ____
- ____
- ____
- ____

  A joint-application design (JAD) session is ______________________

  ____

- ____

II. What initiates the system development life cycle? [p. 14.10]

A user may request a new or modified information system for a variety of reasons, such as to correct a problem, to comply with a mandated change, or to respond to competitors.

A request for system services, or project request, is a formal request for a new or modified information system and becomes ______________________________

____

III. Planning phase [p. 14.12]

The planning phase begins ______________________________

Major activities during the planning phase:

(1) ______________________________

(2) ______________________________

(3) ______________________________

(4) ______________________________

IV. Analysis phase [p. 14.13]

The analysis phase consists of two major tasks:

(1) ______________________________

(2) ______________________________

A. The preliminary investigation [p. 14.13]

The preliminary investigation is ______________________________

____

In this phase, the systems analyst must ______________________________

____

A feasibility report presents the results of the preliminary investigation.

B. Detailed analysis [p. 14.15]

Detailed analysis involves three major activities:

(1) ______________________________

(2) ______________________________

(3) ______________________________

Detailed analysis sometimes is called logical design because ______________

____

C. Structured analysis and design tools [p. 14.15]

Structured analysis and design is ______________________________

____

Structured analysis and design tools:

1. Entity-relationship diagrams [p. 14.16]

An entity-relationship diagram (ERD) is ______________________________

____

An entity is ______________________________

2. Data flow diagrams [p. 14.17]

   A data flow diagram (DFD) is ______________________________

   ____

   Components of a DFD:

   - A data flow shows ______________________________
   - A process transforms ______________________________
   - A data store is ______________________________
   - A source identifies ______________________________

   A context diagram (the top level DFD) identifies ______________________________

   ____

3. Project dictionary [p. 14.17]

   The project dictionary contains ______________________________

   ____

   In the project dictionary, entries from DFDs and ERDs are described using several techniques, including structured English, decision tables and decision trees, and the data dictionary.

4. Structured English [p. 14.18]

   Structured English is ______________________________

   ____

5. Decision tables and decision trees [p. 14.18]

   A decision table is ______________________________

   ____

   A decision tree shows ______________________________

6. Data dictionary [p. 14.19]

   The data dictionary section of the project dictionary stores ______________________________

   ____

D. The system proposal [p. 14.19]

   The system proposal assesses ______________________________

   ____

   When discussing the system proposal, the steering committee often must decide whether to buy packaged software or build custom software.

   1. Packaged software [p. 14.19]

      Packaged software is ______________________________

      ____

      - Horizontal market software is ______________________________
      - Vertical market software is ______________________________

Sources of packaged software can be found on the Web or in trade publications, which are ______________________________

2. Custom software [p. 14.20]

   Custom software is ______________________________

   ____

   The advantage of custom software is ______________________________

   The disadvantage of custom software is ______________________________

3. Solutions providers [p. 14.21]

   Some companies hire solution providers to handle part or all of their IT operations.

V. Design phase [p. 14.21]

The design phase consists of two major activities:

(1) ______________________________

(2) ______________________________

A. Acquiring necessary hardware and software [p. 14.21]

Acquiring the necessary hardware and software consists of four tasks:

(1) ______________________________

(2) ______________________________

(3) ______________________________

(4) ______________________________

B. Identifying technical specifications [p. 14.22]

A systems analyst uses a variety of techniques to identify the hardware and software requirements for a system, such as researching on the Internet.

An e-zine is ______________________________

Technical requirements are summarized using three basic techniques:

- A request for quotation (RFQ) identifies ______________________________

  ____

- A request for proposal (RFP) selects ______________________________

  ____

- A request for information (RFI) is ______________________________

  ____

The RFQ, RFP, and RFI are sent to potential hardware and software vendors.

C. Soliciting vendor proposals [p. 14.23]

Proposals can be solicited from vendors on the Internet, local computer stores, computer manufacturers, or value-added resellers.

A value-added reseller (VAR) is ____

____

A VAR may offer user support, equipment maintenance, training, installation, warranties, and turnkey solutions.

A warranty is ____

A turnkey solution is ____

D. Testing and evaluating vendor proposals [p. 14.24]

Vendor proposals should be rated as objectively as possible.

A benchmark test measures ____

E. Making a decision [p. 14.25]

After rating proposals, the systems analyst makes a recommendation to the steering committee. A contract then can be awarded to a vendor.

An end-user license agreement (EULA) gives ______________________________

____

F. Detailed design [p. 14.26]

Detailed design sometimes is called physical design because ______________

____

Designs are developed for databases, inputs, outputs, and programs.

1. Database design [p. 14.27]

   During database design, the systems analyst builds ____________________

   ____

   ____

2. Input and output design [p. 14.27]

   During input and output design, the systems analyst designs ___________

   ____

   - A mockup is ____
   - A layout chart is ____

3. Program design [p. 14.28]

   During program design, the systems analyst identifies _______________

   ____

   - The program specification package communicates _______________

     ____

   - A systems flowchart documents ______________________________

     ____

G. Prototyping [p. 14.28]

A prototype is ______________________________

____

The process of developing applications with prototypes is part of rapid application development (RAD).

H. CASE tools [p. 14.29]

Computer-aided software engineering (CASE) products are ______________

____

Capabilities of I-CASE (integrated CASE) products:

- ______________
- ______________
- ______________
- ______________
- ______________
- ______________

I. Quality review techniques [p. 14.30]

A structured walkthrough is ______________________________

____

VI. Implementation phase [p. 14.30]

The purpose of the implementation phase is ______________________

____

Four major activities are performed in the implementation phase:

(1) ______________________________

(2) ______________________________

(3) ______________________________

(4) ______________________________

A. Develop programs [p. 14.30]

Custom software can be developed from the specifications created during analysis using a set of activities known as the program development life cycle. The program development life cycle (PDLC) follows six steps:

(1) ______________ (4) ______________

(2) ______________ (5) ______________

(3) ______________ (6) ______________

The PDLC is ______________________________

B. Install and test the new system [p. 14.30]

Types of tests performed to test the new system:

- Systems test — ______________________________

  ____

- Integration test — ______________________________

  ____

- Acceptance test — ______________________________

  ____

C. Train users [p. 14.31]

Training involves ______________________________

D. Convert to the new system [p. 14.31]

Conversion can take place using the following strategies:

- With direct conversion, the user stops ______________________________

  ____

- With parallel conversion, the old system runs ______________________________

  ____

- With a phased conversion, each site converts ______________________________

  ____

- With a pilot conversion, only one location uses ______________________________

  ____

At the beginning of the conversion, data conversion is ______________________________

____

VII. Support phase [p. 14.32]

The purpose of the support phase is ______________________________

____

The support phase consists of four major activities:

(1) ______________________________

(2) ______________________________

(3) ______________________________

(4) ______________________________

The post-implementation system review is ______________________________

____

System enhancement involves ______________________________

____

Performance monitoring is ______________________________

____

Self Test

Matching

1. ____ SDLC
2. ____ ERD
3. ____ DFD
4. ____ RFQ
5. ____ RFP
6. ____ RFI
7. ____ VAR
8. ____ RAD
9. ____ CASE
10. ____ PDLC

a. organized set of six activities in the creation of a computer program
b. standard form sent to vendors to request information about a product or service
c. company that purchases products and resells them along with additional services
d. set of activities that developers use to build an information system
e. uses the process of developing applications with prototypes
f. license agreement granting the right to use software under certain terms and conditions
g. tool that graphically shows the flow of data in a system
h. sent to vendors to identify the products you want and request prices
i. tabular representation of actions to be taken given various conditions
j. computer-based tools designed to support activities of the SDLC
k. tool that graphically shows the connections between entities in a system
l. asks vendors to select products that meet your requirements and then quote prices

True/False

____ 1. The goal of project management is to deliver an acceptable system to the user in an agreed-upon time frame, while maintaining costs.

____ 2. Documentation should be an ongoing part of the system development life cycle.

____ 3. The interview is the least important data and information gathering technique.

____ 4. The perceived problem or enhancement identified in the project request always is the actual problem.

____ 5. An important benefit from using all of the data and information gathering techniques is that these activities build valuable relationships among the systems analyst and users.

____ 6. Lower-level data flow diagrams (DFDs) identify only the major process; that is, the system being studied.

____ 7. Vertical market software packages tend to be widely available because a large number of companies use them; thus, they usually are less expensive than horizontal market software packages.

____ 8. The advantage of a full-source VAR (value-added reseller) is that you deal with only one company for an entire system.

____ 9. The main advantage of a prototype is that users can work with the system before it is completed — to make sure it meets their needs.

____ 10. Errors in an information system may be caused by problems with design (logic) or programming (syntax).

Multiple Choice

____ 1. Which of the following is *not* a general guideline for system development?
a. set constraints
b. use phases
c. involve users
d. develop standards

____ 2. What criteria that tests the feasibility of a project addresses the question of whether users will like the new system?
a. cost/benefit feasibility
b. technical feasibility
c. schedule feasibility
d. operational feasibility

____ 3. What is a reason for requesting a new or modified information system?
a. to comply with a mandated change
b. to respond to competitors
c. to correct a problem
d. all of the above

____ 4. The preliminary investigation is a major task in what phase?
a. analysis
b. planning
c. design
d. implementation

____ 5. In a data flow diagram, what is drawn as a circle?
a. a data flow
b. a process
c. a data store
d. a source

____ 6. What technique graphically represents a variety of conditions and the actions that correspond to each?
a. a project dictionary
b. a decision tree
c. a data dictionary
d. a decision table

____ 7. What is the main advantage of custom software?
a. it matches an organization's requirements exactly
b. it is less expensive than packaged software
c. it takes less time to design than packaged software
d. it takes less time to implement than packaged software

____ 8. What do most end-user license agreements state?
a. software may be used on more than one computer or by more than one user
b. software may not be used on more than one computer, but it can be used by more than one user
c. software may be used on more than one computer but not by more than one user
d. software may not be used on more than one computer or by more than one user

____ 9. What capability is *not* included in I-CASE products?
a. graphics that enable the drawing of diagrams
b. quality assurance that analyzes deliverables
c. generators that produce design specifications from actual programs
d. prototypes that create models of a proposed system

____ 10. An accounting system, with the accounts receivable, accounts payable, general ledger, and payroll sites all being converted in separate stages, would be an example of what kind of conversion?
a. direct conversion
b. parallel conversion
c. phased conversion
d. pilot conversion

Fill in the Blanks

1. To help organize the process, SDLCs often group many activities into larger categories called ____________________.
2. To plan and schedule a project effectively, the project leader must identify the goal, objectives, and expectations of the project, called the ____________________.
3. A document called a(n) ____________________ becomes the first item in the project notebook and triggers the first phase in the SDLC.
4. A report called a(n) ____________________ compiles the findings of a very general preliminary investigation.

5. In a data flow diagram, a(n) ____________________ is drawn as a square and identifies an entity outside the scope of the system that sends data into the system or receives information from the system.

6. The goal of the ____________________ is to assess the feasibility of each alternative solution and then recommend the most feasible solution for the development project.

7. ____________________ is application software developed by the user or at the user's request.

8. A(n) ____________________ is a guarantee that a product will function properly for a specified period of time.

9. ____________________ users to use the new hardware and software in a system could be one-on-one sessions or classroom-style lectures.

10. Converting existing manual and computer-based files so they can be used by a new system is known as ____________________.

Complete the Table

CONVERTING TO A NEW SYSTEM

Conversion Strategy	*time* →		
____________________	old system		____________________
Parallel Conversion	____________________		
		____________________	
____________________	____________________	new system	
		pilot site	
	old system	old system	new system
____________________	old system	old system	new system
	______________	new system	new system

Things to Think About

1. Why does the start of many activities in the system development life cycle depend on the successful completion of other activities?

2. Although they are created in the analysis phase, how might the project dictionary and data dictionary be used in subsequent phases of the system development life cycle?

3. If an organization chooses to buy packaged software, why might it have to change some of its methods and procedures? When might custom software be worth the additional cost and development time?
4. How can untrained users prevent the estimated benefits of a new system from ever being obtained or, worse, contribute to less efficiency and more costs than when the old system was operational?

Puzzle

Write the word described by each clue in the puzzle below. Words can be written forward or backward, across, up and down, or diagonally. The initial letter of each word already appears in the puzzle.

S											D
										A	
	D		S							V	
			I	W							
		P			C						
										P	
		E					G				
				R						D	
								S			R
			S								P
											R
P				E							F

Set of activities developers use to build an information system

Sets of rules and procedures a company expects employees to follow

Formed to work on a development project from beginning to end

Manages and controls the budget and schedule of a project

Type of horizontal bar chart that shows time relationship of project activities

Tangible item such as a chart, diagram, report, or program file

Measure of how suitable development of a system will be to a company

Phase in which the project request is reviewed and approved

Phase in which detailed analysis is performed

Tool that graphically shows connections between entities in a project

Tool that graphically shows the flow of data in a system

In a data flow diagram, it is represented by a line with an arrow

In a data flow diagram, it is represented by a rectangle with no sides

In a data flow diagram, it is represented by a square

Contains all the documentation and deliverables of a project

Type of software developed by the user or at the user's request

Identifies the products you want from a vendor

Vendor selection of products that meet requirements

Less formal method that uses a standard form to request product information

Guarantee that a product will function properly for a specified time period

Company that purchases products and resells them with additional services

Gives the legal right to use software under certain terms and conditions

Working model of a proposed system used during detailed design

Organized set of activities used in program development

Type of conversion in which only one location uses the new system

Phase in which a post-implementation system review is conducted

Self Test Answers

Matching

1. *d* [p. 14.02]
2. *k* [p. 14.16]
3. *g* [p. 14.17]
4. *h* [p. 14.22]
5. *l* [p. 14.23]
6. *b* [p. 14.23]
7. *c* [p. 14.23]
8. *e* [p. 14.28]
9. *j* [p. 14.29]
10. *a* [p. 14.30]

True/False

1. *T* [p. 14.05]
2. *T* [p. 14.07]
3. *F* [p. 14.07]
4. *F* [p. 14.13]
5. *T* [p. 14.15]
6. *F* [p. 14.17]
7. *F* [p. 14.20]
8. *T* [p. 14.24]
9. *T* [p. 14.28]
10. *T* [p. 14.32]

Multiple Choice

1. *a* [p. 14.03]
2. *d* [p. 14.06]
3. *d* [p. 14.10]
4. *a* [p. 14.13]
5. *b* [p. 14.17]
6. *b* [p. 14.18]
7. *a* [p. 14.21]
8. *d* [p. 14.26]
9. *c* [p. 14.29]
10. *c* [p. 14.32]

Fill in the Blanks

1. *phases* [p. 14.02]
2. *scope* [p. 14.05]
3. *request for system services* or *project request* [p. 14.10]
4. *feasibility study* or *feasibility report* [p. 14.13]
5. *source* or *agent* [p. 14.17]
6. *system proposal* [p. 14.19]
7. *Custom software* [p. 14.20]
8. *warranty* [p. 14.23]
9. *Training* [p. 14.30]
10. *data conversion* [p. 14.32]

Complete the Table

CONVERTING TO A NEW SYSTEM

Conversion Strategy	*time* →		
Direct Conversion	old system		*new system*
Parallel Conversion	*old system*	*old system*	
		new system	*new system*
Phased Conversion	*old system*	new system	new system
		pilot site	
Pilot Conversion	old system	old system	new system
	old system	old system	new system
	new system	new system	new system

Things to Think About

Answers will vary.

Puzzle Answer

S	T	A	N	D	A	R	D	S		R	**D**
N	Y		S	I	S	Y	L	A	N	**A**	E
A	**D**	T	**S**	U	P	P	O	R	T	**V**	P
L	A	F	**I**	**W**	A	R	R	A	N	T	Y
P	T	**P**	D	L	**C**	U	S	T	O	M	T
T	A	I	U	Q	I	T	O	L	I	**P**	O
C	F	**E**	F	F	O	B	**G**	A	N	T	T
E	L	B	A	**R**	E	V	I	L	E	**D**	O
J	O	D	E	C	R	U	O	**S**	P	F	**R**
O	W	D	**S**	G	N	I	N	N	A	L	**P**
R		Y	R	O	T	I	S	O	P	E	**R**
P	R	O	J	**E**	C	T	T	E	A	M	**F**

DISCOVERING COMPUTERS 2003

STUDY GUIDE

CHAPTER 15

Program Development and Programming Languages

Chapter Overview

This chapter discusses each step in the program development life cycle and presents the tools used to make this process efficient. You learn about various programming languages and the program development tools used to write and develop computer programs. Finally, the chapter presents a variety of Web development and multimedia development tools.

Chapter Objectives

After completing this chapter, you should be able to:

- Explain the six steps in the program development life cycle
- Describe top-down program design
- Explain structured program design and the three basic control structures
- Explain the differences among the categories of programming languages
- Describe the object-oriented approach to program development
- Identify programming languages commonly used today
- Identify the uses of application generators, macros, and RAD tools
- Describe various Web page development tools, including HTML, DHTML, XML, and WML
- Identify uses of multimedia authoring packages

Chapter Outline

I. What is a computer program? [p. 15.02]

A computer program is ____

____

II. The program development life cycle [p. 15.02]

The program development life cycle (PDLC) is ______________________

____

The PDLC consists of six steps:

1. ____________ 3. ____________ 5. ____________

2. ____________ 4. ____________ 6. ____________

The phases form a loop; that is, program development is an ongoing process within the SDLC.

A. What initiates the program development life cycle? [p. 15.03]

A company may opt for in-house development of custom software.

A program specification package identifies ____________

____

The PDLC begins at the start of the implementation phase of the SDLC.

A programming team consists ____________

____

III. Step 1 – Analyze Problem [p. 15.04]

The analysis step consists of three major tasks:

(1) ____________

(2) ____________

(3) ____________

An IPO chart identifies ____________

____

IV. Step 2 – Design Programs [p. 15.05]

Designing programs involves three tasks:

(1) ____________

(2) ____________

(3) ____________

A. Top-down design [p. 15.05]

Top-down design breaks ____________

____

- The main routine is ____________
- Subroutines are ____________
- A module is ____________
- The main module is ____________

A hierarchy chart shows ____________

B. Structured design [p. 15.06]

Structured design is ____________

____

A control structure is ____

____

Structured design uses three basic control structures:

1. Sequence control structure [p. 15.06]

   A sequence control structure shows ______________________________

   ____

2. Selection control structure [p. 15.07]

   A selection control structure tells _______________________________

   ____

   Common types of selection control structures:

   - An if-then-else control structure yields ____________________

     ____

   - The case control structure can yield _______________________

     ____

3. The repetition control structure [p. 15.08]

   The repetition control structure is used ______________________

   ____

   Forms of the repetition control structure:

   - The do-while control structure repeats ____________________

     ____

   - The do-until control structure is __________________________

     ____

C. Proper program design [p. 15.08]

With top-down and structured techniques, programmers must ensure that programs adhere to proper program design rules. A proper program has:

1. No dead code

   Dead code is ____

2. No infinite loops

   An infinite loop is _______________________________________

3. One entry point

   An entry point is ____

4. One exit point

   An exit point is ____

Spaghetti code is ____

D. Design tools [p. 15.09]

Program logic, or a solution algorithm is ______________________________

____

Design tools help to develop a solution algorithm. Three design tools are program flowcharts, Nassi-Schneiderman charts, and pseudocode.

1. Program flowchart [p. 15.09]

   A program flowchart graphically shows ______________________________

   ____

   A comment symbol explains ______________________________________

   Programmers use flowcharting software to develop flowcharts.

2. Nassi-Schneiderman chart [p. 15.11]

   A Nassi-Schneiderman (N-S) chart graphically shows ________________

   ____

   N-S charts sometimes are called structured flowcharts because __________

   ____

3. Pseudocode [p. 15.12]

   Pseudocode uses ____

   ____

E. Quality review techniques [p. 15.12]

During a quality review, the programmer checks ______________________

____

A logic error is ____

A desk check uses ____

____

Test data is ____

Desk checking involves five steps:

1. ____
2. ____
3. ____
4. ____
5. ____

V. Step 3 – Code Programs [p. 15.13]

Coding programs involves two steps:

(1) ____

(2) ____

Syntax is ______________________________

Comments are ______________________________

- Global comments explain ______________________________
- Internal comments explain ______________________________

VI. Step 4 – Test Programs [p. 15.13]

The goal of program testing is ______________________________

____

Errors usually are one of two types:

(1) ______________________ (2) ______________________

A syntax error occurs ______________________________

The procedure for testing for logic errors is much like desk checking.

Run time errors make ______________________________

Debugging is ______________________________

- Bugs are ______________________________
- A debug utility allows ______________________________

VII. Step 5 – Formalize Solution [p. 15.15]

In formalizing the solution, the programmer performs two activities:

(1) ______________________________

(2) ______________________________

VIII. Step 6 – Maintain Programs [p. 15.15]

Maintaining programs involves two activities:

(1) ______________________________

(2) ______________________________

Program enhancement involves ______________________________

____

IX. Programming languages and program development tools [p. 15.16]

A programming language is ______________________________

____

A program development tool consists ______________________________

____

X. Categories of programming languages [p. 15.16]

- A low-level language is ______________________________

  A machine-dependent language runs ______________________________

  Machine and assembly languages are low-level languages.

- A high-level language is ____________________

  A machine-independent language can ____________________

  ____

  Third-generation, fourth-generation, and fifth-generation languages are high-level languages.

A. Machine languages (first-generation language) [p. 15.16]

   Machine language is ____________________

   ____

B. Assembly languages (second-generation languages) [p. 15.16]

   With an assembly language, a programmer writes ____________________

   ____

   Symbolic instruction codes are ____________________

   A symbolic address is ____________________

   A source program is ____________________

   An assembler converts ____________________

   ____

C. Third-generation languages [p. 15.18]

   A third-generation language (3GL) instruction uses ____________________

   ____

   Third-generation languages are procedural languages.

   A procedural language requires ____________________

   ____

   3GL source programs are translated using one of two types of programs:

   - A compiler converts ____________________

     ____

     The object code is ____________________
   - An interpreter reads ____________________

     ____

D. Fourth-generation languages [p. 15.19]

   A fourth-generation language (4GL) uses ____________________

   ____

   A fourth-generation language is a nonprocedural language.

   With a nonprocedural language, a programmer specifies ____________________

   ____

   Many 4GLs work in combination with a database and its project dictionary.

- A query language enables ______________________________

  ____

- A report writer is ______________________________

  ____

E. Fifth-generation languages [p. 15.20]

A fifth-generation language (5GL) is ______________________________

____

XI. Object-oriented program development [p. 15.20]

With the object-oriented approach, the programmer can ______________________________

____

An object is ______________________________

____

- A method contains ______________________________
- An attribute is ______________________________

Encapsulation is ______________________________

A class is ______________________________

- A subclass is ______________________________
- A superclass is ______________________________

Inheritance is ______________________________

An object instance is ______________________________

A message tells ______________________________

A benefit of the OO approach is the ability to reuse and modify existing objects. The Object Management Group (OMG), which establishes guidelines for OO application development, has adopted UML and CORBA as programming standards.

UML (Unified Modeling Language) contains ______________________________

____

The Object Management Group (OMG) is ______________________________

____

CORBA (Common Object Request Broker Architecture) defines ______________________________

____

A. Object-oriented programming [p. 15.21]

An object-oriented programming (OOP) language is ______________________________

____

Event is ______________________________

XII. Programming languages [p. 15.22]

Although there are hundreds of programming languages, only a few are widely used. Most are high-level languages that work on a variety of machines.

A. BASIC [p. 15.22]

____

____

B. Visual Basic [p. 15.22]

____

____

C. COBOL [p. 15.24]

____

____

D. C [p. 15.25]

____

____

E. C++ [p. 15.25]

____

____

C# combines ________________________________

F. RPG [p. 15.26]

____

____

G. Other programming languages [p. 15.26]

____

____

XIII. Program development tools [p. 15.27]

Program development tools are ____________________________

____

In addition to query languages and report writers, program development tools include application generators, macros, and RAD tools.

A. Application generators [p. 15.27]

An application generator is ____________________________

____

A menu generator allows ____________________________

B. Macros [p. 15.28]

A macro is ______________________________

____

You usually create a macro in one of two ways:

(1) ______________________________

A macro recorder is ______________________________

(2) ______________________________

Visual Basic for Applications (VBA) is a popular macro programming language.

C. RAD tools: Visual Basic, Delphi, and PowerBuilder [p. 15.29]

Rapid application development (RAD) is ______________________________

____

RAD tools are used to create easy-to-maintain, component-based applications.

A component is ______________________________

Popular RAD tools:

1. Visual Basic [p. 15.29]

   ____

   A visual programming environment (VPE) allows ______________________________

   ____

2. Delphi [p. 15.29]

   ____

3. PowerBuilder [p. 15.30]

   ____

XIV. Web page program development [p. 15.30]

Web page authors use ______________________________

A. HTML [p. 15.31]

Hypertext Markup Language (HTML) is ______________________________

____

HTML uses tags, which are ______________________________

____

B. Scripts, applets, servlets, and ActiveX controls [p. 15.32]

To add dynamic content and interactive elements to Web pages, you write small programs called scripts, applets, servlets, and Active X controls.

- A script is ______________________________
- An applet usually runs ______________________________

- A servlet is ______________________________
- An ActiveX control is ______________________________

  ActiveX is ______________________________

Interactive capabilities on a Web page:

- A counter tracks ______________________________
- An image map is ______________________________
- A processing form collects ______________________________

The common gateway interface (CGI) is ______________________________

____

A CGI script is ______________________________

C. Java, JavaScript, VBScript, and Perl [p. 15.34]

A scripting language is ______________________________

____

Popular scripting languages:

1. Java [p. 15.34]

   Java is ______________________________

   ____

   JavaBeans are ______________________________

2. JavaScript [p. 15.35]

   JavaScript is ______________________________

   ____

   An open language means ______________________________

3. VBScript [p. 15.36]

   VBScript is ______________________________

   ____

4. Perl [p. 15.36]

   Perl is ______________________________

   ____

D. Dynamic HTML [p. 15.36]

Dynamic HTML (DHTML) is ______________________________

____

DHTML works by using scripting languages, the document object model (DOM), and cascading style sheets (CSS).

- The DOM defines ______________________________
- CSS contain ______________________________

E. XHTML, XML, and WML [p. 15.37]

XHTML (eXtensible HTML) includes features of HTML and XML.

XML (eXtensible Markup Language) allows ______________________________

____

XSL (eXtensible Stylesheet Language) is ______________________________

WML (wireless markup language) allows ______________________________

____

Wireless application protocol (WAP) is ______________________________

____

F. .NET Platform [p. 15.38]

Microsoft's .NET Platform is ______________________________

____

A .NET-compliant smart client is ______________________________

____

Examples of .NET-compliant smart clients:

- Tablet PC is ______________________________
- Xbox™ is ______________________________

Visual Studio .NET (VS.NET) is ______________________________

____

Popular programming languages supported by VS.NET:

- Visual Basic .NET includes ______________________________
- Visual C++® .NET with ______________________________
- Visual C#™ .NET incorporates ______________________________

G. Web page authoring software [p. 15.38]

Web page authoring software allows ______________________________

____

XV. Multimedia Program Development [p. 15.39]

Multimedia authoring software allows ______________________________

____

Developers often use multimedia authoring software for computer-based training (CBT) and Web-based training (WBT) environments.

- CBT is ______________________________
- WBT is ______________________________

WBT, CBT, and other materials often are combined for distance learning courses.

Distance learning is ______________________________

A. ToolBook, Authorware, and Director [p. 15.39]

ToolBook, Authorware, and Director are popular multimedia authoring packages.

1. ToolBook [p. 15.40]

   ToolBook has ______________________________

   ____

2. Authorware [p. 15.40]

   Authorware is ______________________________

   ____

3. Director [p. 15.40]

   Director is ______________________________

   ____

XVI. Selecting a programming language or program development tool [p. 15.40]

Factors to consider:

1. ______________________________
2. ______________________________
3. ______________________________
4. ______________________________

Self Test

Matching

1. ____ BASIC
2. ____ Visual Basic
3. ____ COBOL
4. ____ C
5. ____ RPG
6. ____ HTML
7. ____ Java
8. ____ VBScript
9. ____ Perl
10. ____ XML

a. simple, interactive, problem-solving language sometimes used in introductory courses
b. nonprocedural language used for complex computations and file updating
c. scientific language designed to manipulate tables of numbers
d. object-oriented language developed by Apple to manipulate multimedia cards
e. Windows-based application that assists in developing event-driven applications
f. interpreted scripting language with powerful text processing capabilities
g. scripting language used to add intelligence and interactivity to Web pages
h. widely used procedural language for business applications
i. originally designed as a language for writing systems software, most often used with UNIX
j. compiled object-oriented language used to write applications, applets, and servlets
k. special formatting language that programmers use to create Web pages
l. markup language that allows developers to create customized tags or use predefined tags

True/False

____ 1. Programs developed using the top-down approach suffer from the complexity of their design — they usually are unstable and difficult to read and maintain.

____ 2. A do-until control structure continues looping until the condition is true — and then stops.

____ 3. Some people use the term, spaghetti code, to refer to the poorly designed programs with multiple entry and exit points.

____ 4. During program testing, one purpose of using test data is to try to crash the system; that is, to cause run time errors or make the program fail.

____ 5. A computer can understand and execute an assembler source program.

____ 6. While a compiler translates one program statement at a time, an interpreter translates an entire program at once.

____ 7. When using an application generator, the developer (a programmer or user) works with menu-driven tools that have graphical user interfaces.

____ 8. Many applications use Visual Basic for Applications (VBA) or a similar language as their macro programming language.

____ 9. Scripts, applets, and servlets are long programs that are executed by the operating system — unlike regular programs, which run inside of another program.

____ 10. A Web page written with XML probably would require multiple versions to run on a handheld computer, a notebook computer, and a desktop computer.

Multiple Choice

____ 1. Preparing the program specification package is an activity in what phase of the system development life cycle?
   a. the planning phase
   b. the analysis phase
   c. the design phase
   d. the implementation phase

____ 2. What is the first step in top-down design?
   a. identify the major function of the program
   b. break down the program's main routine into smaller sections
   c. identify the minor functions of the program
   d. combine the program's smaller sections into a main routine

____ 3. Which of the following is *not* a commonly used program design tool?
   a. program flowcharts
   b. Nassi-Schneiderman charts
   c. pseudocode
   d. debug utilities

____ 4. What is the first step in desk checking?
   a. determine the expected result
   b. step through the solution algorithm using test data
   c. compare the expected result to the actual result
   d. develop test data

____ 5. What major category of programming languages uses a series of binary digits (1s and 0s) that correspond to the on and off electrical states of a computer?
   a. machine languages (first-generation language)
   b. assembly languages (second-generation languages)
   c. third-generation languages
   d. fourth-generation languages

____ 6. Because they are nonprocedural, what major category of programming languages tend to be quite easy to use?
   a. machine languages (first-generation language)
   b. assembly languages (second-generation languages)
   c. third-generation languages
   d. fourth-generation languages

____ 7. What is C++?
   a. a language similar to C used for device control applications
   b. an object-oriented extension of C used to develop application software
   c. a successor to C used for artificial intelligence applications
   d. an enhanced version of C with features of COBOL

____ 8. Although a version with limited functionality is available for the personal computer, what programming language primarily is used for application development on IBM midrange computers?
   a. BASIC
   b. RPG
   c. HTML
   d. COBOL

____ 9. What are <B> to bold text, <P> to indicate a new paragraph, and <HR> to display a horizontal rule across a page?
   a. scripts
   b. applets
   c. tags
   d. servlets

____ 10. What is *not* a factor that should be considered when selecting a programming language?
   a. standards of the organization
   b. need for testing and documentation
   c. suitability of the language to the application
   d. portability to other systems

Fill in the Blanks

1. In a program flowchart, dotted lines are used to connect ____________________, which explain or clarify logic in the solution algorithm.
2. Today, programmers use ____________________ to develop flowcharts, which it easy to modify and update flowcharts.
3. A program has its own documentation, called ____________________.
4. The ____________________, which took effect when the computer date rolled over to January 1, 2000, had the potential to cause serious financial losses.
5. Once programs are ____________________, or placed into production, users interact with the programs.
6. Assembly languages use ____________________, which are meaningful names that identify storage locations.
7. In some cases, assembly languages include ____________________, which generate multiple machine language instructions.
8. SQL is a(n) ____________________ enabling users and programmers to retrieve data from database tables.

9. Program development tools ____________________ nontechnical users by giving them the ability to write simple programs and satisfy information requests on their own.
10. Unlike C++, Java source code is compiled into ____________________, instead of object code.

Complete the Table

ANSI FLOWCHART SYMBOLS

Symbol	Operation/Purpose
	____________________ program instruction(s) that transforms input(s) into output(s)
____________	INPUT/OUTPUT ______________________________________
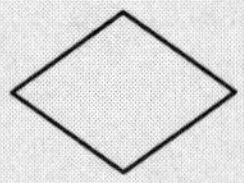	____________________ condition that determines a specified path to follow
____________	TERMINAL ______________________________________
	____________________ entry from or exit to another part of the flowchart on same page
____________	CONNECTOR ______________________________________
	____________________ named process containing a series of program steps specified elsewhere

Things to Think About

1. Why should a programmer not change design specifications without the agreement of the systems analyst and the user?
2. Prior to the introduction of structured program design, programmers focused on the detailed steps required for a program and logical solutions for each new combination of conditions as it was encountered. Why would developing programs in this manner lead to these poorly designed programs?
3. Why is it better to find errors and make needed changes to a program during the design step than to make them later in the development process?
4. Would it be more difficult to uncover syntax errors or logic errors in a program? Why?

Puzzle

The terms described by the phrases below are written below each line in code. Break the code by writing the correct term above the coded word. Then, use your broken code to translate the final sentence.

1. Set of instructions that directs the computer to perform tasks — EJGCWMZD CDJUDHG
2. Identifies a program's inputs, its outputs, and the processing steps required — IZOSBSBU ISHUDHG
3. Used by programmers to represent program modules graphically — MJC-IJRB EYHDM
4. Technique that builds all program logic from a combination of three control structures — QMDWEMWDZI IZQSUB
5. Design that determines the logical order of program instructions — EJBQMDWEM
6. Type of control structure that shows one or more actions following each other in order — QZXWZBEZ
7. Type of control structure used when a program performs one or more actions repeatedly — SMZDHMSJB
8. What Nassi-Schneiderman (N-S) charts sometimes are called — QMDWEMWDZI OVJREYHDMQ
9. Documentation within a program, identified by the letters REM in QuickBASIC — DZGHDFQ
10. Utility that identifies syntax errors and finds logic errors in a program — IZAWUUZD
11. Error that had the potential to cause financial losses for computers at the turn of the century — P2F AWU
12. Meaningful abbreviations for assembly language program instructions — GBZGJBSEQ
13. Software that allows you to design or layout a report on the screen and then print it — DZCJDM UZBZDHMJD
14. In the object-oriented approach, the procedures in an object — JCZDHMSJBQ
15. In the object-oriented approach, the data elements in an object — KHDSHAVZQ
16. Development tool that allows you to build an application without writing extensive code — CDJUDHG UZBZDHMJD

17. HTML codes that specify links to other documents and how a Web page displays	______________ GHDFWCQ
18. Collects data from visitors to a Web site, who fill in blank fields	______________ CDJEZQQSBU OJDG
19. Simple, open scripting language that anyone can use without purchasing a license	______________ THKHQEDSCM
20. Web page development language that can be used to define a link to multiple Web sites	______________ ZLMZBQSAVZ GHDFWC

MJ VWDZ ZLCZDM CDJUDHGGZDQ, SB HIISMSJB MJ YSUY QHVHDSZQ HBI

QSUBSBU AJBWQZQ QJGZ EJGCHBSZQ HDZ JOOZDSBU QWEY CZDFQ HQ

OVZLSAVZ YJWDQ, IHP EHDZ, OHGSVP VZHKZ, QMJEF JCMSJBQ, RJDFCVHEZ

OSMBZQQ EZBMZDQ, HBI ZKZB QWAQSISNZI VHWBIDP QZDKSEZ.

Self Test Answers

Matching

1. *a* [p. 15.22]
2. *e* [p. 15.22]
3. *h* [p. 15.24]
4. *i* [p. 15.25]
5. *b* [p. 15.26]
6. *k* [p. 15.31]
7. *j* [p. 15.34]
8. *g* [p. 15.36]
9. *f* [p. 15.36]
10. *l* [p. 15.37]

True/False

1. *F* [p. 15.06]
2. *F* [p. 15.08]
3. *T* [p. 15.09]
4. *T* [p. 15.13]
5. *F* [p. 15.17]
6. *F* [p. 15.18]
7. *T* [p. 15.27]
8. *T* [p. 15.28]
9. *F* [p. 15.32]
10. *F* [p. 15.37]

Multiple Choice

1. *c* [p. 15.03]
2. *a* [p. 15.05]
3. *d* [p. 15.09]
4. *d* [p. 15.12]
5. *a* [p. 15.16]
6. *d* [p. 15.19]
7. *b* [p. 15.25]
8. *b* [p. 15.26]
9. *c* [p. 15.31]
10. *b* [p. 15.40]

Fill in the Blanks

1. *comment symbols* or *annotation symbols* [p. 15.10]
2. *flowcharting software* [p. 15.10]
3. *comments* or *remarks* [p. 15.13]
4. *millennium bug* or *Y2K bug* [p. 15.14]
5. *implemented* [p. 15.15]
6. *symbolic addresses* [p. 15.16]
7. *macros* [p. 15.17]
8. *query language* [p. 15.18]
9. *empower* [p. 15.27]
10. *bytecode* [p. 15.34]

Complete the Table

ANSI FLOWCHART SYMBOLS

Symbol	Operation/Purpose
	*PROCESS* program instruction(s) that transforms input(s) into output(s)
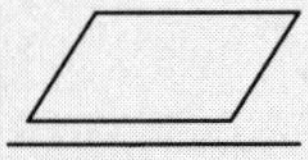	INPUT/OUTPUT *enter data or display information*
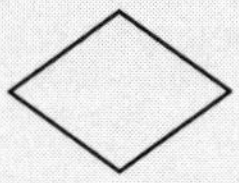	*DECISION* condition that determines a specified path to follow
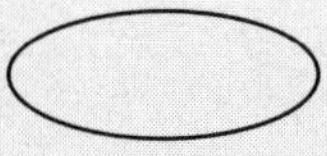	TERMINAL *beginning or end of program*

Symbol	Operation/Purpose
	*CONNECTOR* entry from or exit to another part of flowchart on same page
	CONNECTOR *entry from or exit to another part of flowchart on different page*
	*PREDEFINED PROCESS* named process containing a series of program steps specified elsewhere

Things to Think About

Answers will vary.

Puzzle Answer

1.	Set of instructions that directs the computer to perform tasks	*computer program* EJGCWMZD CDJUDHG
2.	Identifies a program's inputs, its outputs, and the processing steps required	*defining diagram* IZOSBSBU ISHUDHG
3.	Used by programmers to represent program modules graphically	*top-down chart* MJC-IJRB EYHDM
4.	Technique that builds all program logic from a combination of three control structures	*structured design* QMDWEMWDZI IZQSUB
5.	Design that determines the logical order of program instructions	*construct* EJBQMDWEM
6.	Type of control structure that shows one or more actions following each other in order	*sequence* QZXWZBEZ
7.	Type of control structure used when a program performs one or more actions repeatedly	*iteration* SMZDHMSJB
8.	What Nassi-Schneiderman (N-S) charts sometimes are called	*structured flowcharts* QMDWEMWDZI OVJREYHDMQ
9.	Documentation within a program, identified by the letters REM in QuickBASIC	*remarks* DZGHDFQ
10.	Utility that identifies syntax errors and finds logic errors in a program	*debugger* IZAWUUZD
11.	Error that had the potential to cause financial losses for computers at the turn of the century	*Y2K Bug* P2F AWU

12. Meaningful abbreviations for assembly language program instructions — *mnemonics*
GBZGJBSEQ

13. Software that allows you to design or layout a report on the screen and then print it — *report generator*
DZCJDM UZBZDHMJD

14. In the object-oriented approach, the procedures in an object — *operations*
JCZDHMSJBQ

15. In the object-oriented approach, the data elements in an object — *variables*
KHDSHAVZQ

16. Development tool that allows you to build an application without writing extensive code — *program generator*
CDJUDHG UZBZDHMJD

17. HTML codes that specify links to other documents and how a Web page displays — *markups*
GHDFWCQ

18. Collects data from visitors to a Web site, who fill in blank fields — *processing form*
CDJEZQQSBU OJDG

19. Simple, open scripting language that anyone can use without purchasing a license — *JavaScript*
THKHQEDSCM

20. Web page development language that can be used to define a link to multiple Web sites — *eXtensible Markup*
ZLMZBQSAVZ GHDFWC

To lure expert programmers, in addition to high salaries and
MJ VWDZ ZLCZDM CDJUDHGGZDQ, SB HIISMSJB MJ YSUY QHVHDSZQ HBI

signing bonuses some companies are offering such perks as
QSUBSBU AJBWQZQ QJGZ EJGCHBSZQ HDZ JOOZDSBU QWEY CZDFQ HQ

flexible hours, day care, family leave, stock options, workplace
OVZLSAVZ YJWDQ, IHP EHDZ, OHGSVP VZHKZ, QMJEF JCMSJBQ, RJDFCVHEZ

fitness centers, and even subsidized laundry service.
OSMBZQQ EZBMZDQ, HBI ZKZB QWAQSISNZI VHWBIDP QZDKSEZ.

NOTES

DISCOVERING COMPUTERS 2003

STUDY GUIDE

CHAPTER 16

Computer Careers and Certification

Chapter Overview

This chapter discusses the strong demand for computer and IT professionals. You learn about available careers, job preparation, and career development planning. The chapter also provides information about certification preparation, examinations, and resources. Finally, career development after certification is discussed.

Chapter Objectives

After completing this chapter, you should be able to:

- Describe career opportunities in the computer industry
- Discuss how to prepare for a career in the computer industry
- Define the term certification
- Describe types of IT certification
- List the benefits of certification
- Explain considerations for choosing a certification
- Describe methods of preparation for certification
- Discuss features of certification examinations and recertification requirements
- Understand how to keep informed about changes in certification

Chapter Outline

I. Careers in the computer industry [p. 16.02]

Job opportunities in the computer industry are found primarily in four areas:

- ______________________________
- ______________________________
- ______________________________
- ______________________________

The computer industry also includes service companies that support these areas.

A. The computer equipment industry [p. 16.04]

The computer equipment industry consists ______________________________

____

Computer equipment manufacturers include: ______________________

____

B. The computer software industry [p. 16.04]

The computer software industry is ______________________

____

Leading software companies include: ______________________

____

Computer software industry positions:

- Programmer/analyst ______________________

  ____

- Project developer ______________________

  ____

- Software engineer ______________________

  ____

C. Computer careers in business and government [p. 16.06]

In businesses and governmental agencies, the IT department employs _______

____

D. Computer career opportunities [p. 16.06]

Thousands of high-tech jobs have been created as a result of an increasing dependency on computers and the Internet.

Internet industry positions:

- Electronic commerce specialist ______________________

  ____

- Web administrator ______________________

  ____

- Web developer ______________________

  ____

- Web graphic designer ______________________

  ____

- Web programmer ______________________

  ____

- Webcaster ______________________

  ____

- Webmaster ______________________

  ____

E. Working in an IT department [p. 16.08]

Generally, the jobs in an IT department fall into five major groups:

1. The management group directs ________________________________

____

2. The operations group is ________________________________

____

3. The system development group is ________________________________

____

4. The technical services group is ________________________________

____

5. The end-user computing group is ________________________________

____

Information technology positions:

Management

- MIS director/CIO ________________________________

  ____

- Project leader ________________________________

  ____

- Project manager ________________________________

  ____

Operations

- Computer operator ________________________________

  ____

- Data communications analyst ________________________________

  ____

- Network (LAN) administrator ________________________________

  ____

System development

- Application programmer ________________________________

  ____

- Computer science engineer/software engineer ________________________________

  ____

- Technical writer ________________________________

  ____

- Systems analyst ________________________________

  ____

Technical services

- Database analyst/data modeler ______________________________

  ____

- Desktop publishing specialist ______________________________

  ____

- Graphic designer/illustrator ______________________________

  ____

- Network security specialist ______________________________

  ____

- Quality assurance specialist ______________________________

  ____

- Systems programmer ______________________________

  ____

End-user computing

- Computer technician/computer service technician ______________

  ____

- Help desk specialist ______________________________

  ____

F. The computer education and training industry [p. 16.10]
   A high demand exists in schools and industry for qualified instructors who can teach IT subjects.

G. Computing careers in sales [p. 16.10]
   Sales representatives must ______________________________

   ____

H. Computing careers in service and repair [p. 16.10]
   A service and repair technician is ______________________________

   ____

I. Consulting in the computer industry [p. 16.11]
   Consultants must ______________________________

   ____

   ____

II. Preparing for a career in the computer industry [p. 16.11]
   To prepare for a career in the computer industry, you must decide on the area in which you are interested and then obtain education in that field.

A. Choosing the right course of study [p. 16.12]

Three broad disciplines in higher education produce the majority of entry-level employees in the computer industry.

- Computer information systems (CIS) programs emphasize ____________

  ____

- Computer science (CS) programs stress ____________________

  ____

- Computer engineering (CE) programs teach ________________

  ____

B. Attending a trade school [p. 16.13]

Trade schools offer ______________________________________

____

C. Planning for career development [p. 16.14]

Computer professionals must keep up to date on industry trends and technology, develop new skills, and increase recognition among peers. Professional organizations, professional growth and continuing education activities, computer publications, and certification are ways to achieve these objectives.

D. Professional organizations [p. 16.14]

Two influential professional organizations in the computer industry are:

- The Association for Computing Machinery (ACM) is_____________

  ____

- The Association of Information Technology Professionals (AITP) is _____

  ____

A user group is ____________________________________

____

E. Professional growth and continuing education [p. 16.14]

Workshops, seminars, conferences, conventions, and trade shows provide both general and specific information on computer equipment, software, services, and issues.

COMDEX brings ____________________________________

____

F. Computer publications [p. 16.15]

Hundreds of computer industry publications are available. Some cover a wide range of issues, while others are oriented toward a particular topic. Many publications also have Web sites.

III. What is certification? [p. 16.16]

Certification is ______________________________

____

Benefits of certification include:

- ______________________________
- ______________________________
- ______________________________

IV. Types of certification [p. 16.16]

More than 200 certifications are available. Some certifications have a broad focus, while others require an in-depth knowledge of a single computing aspect.

V. A guide to certification [p. 16.17]

Certifications are categorized by their role in the IT industry: software applications, operating systems, programming, hardware, networks, the Internet, and database systems.

A. Software application certifications [p. 16.18]

____

____

B. Operating system certifications [p. 16.18]

____

____

C. Programming certifications [p. 16.18]

____

____

D. Hardware certifications [p. 16.20]

____

____

E. Networking certifications [p. 16.20]

____

____

F. Internet certifications [p. 16.22]

____

____

G. Database system certifications [p. 16.24]

____

____

VI. Certification benefits [p. 16.24]

Certification benefits employees, customers, employers, and the entire computer industry.

Benefits and beneficiaries of certification:

- Employees

  Career ______________________________

  ____

  Professional ______________________________

  ____

  Salary ______________________________

  ____

- Customers ______________________________

  ____

- Employers ______________________________

  ____

- Industry ______________________________

  ____

VII. Choosing a certification [p. 16.27]

Selecting a certification requires careful thought and research.

Factors to consider when selecting a certification:

- ______________________________
- ______________________________
- ______________________________
- ______________________________
- ______________________________
- ______________________________

VIII. Preparing for certification [p. 16.28]

Certification training options are available to suit every learning style.

- Self-Study ______________________________

  ____

  ____

- Online Training ______________________________

  Classes ______________________________

  ____

- Instructor-Led Training ______________________________
____
____
- Web Resources ______________________________
____
____

IX. Certification examinations [p. 16.29]
Authorized testing companies provide most certification exams. Most tests are taken using computers so results are known immediately. Some tests use computerized adaptive testing (CAT), which analyzes ______________________
____
Occasionally, a certification requires a hands-on lab test.

X. Career development after certification [p. 16.30]
Certification sponsors often provide restricted-access Web resources specifically for certificate holders. Most certifications expire after a set time period because product-based skills remain current for only about 18 months. Sponsors specify training or examinations to maintain the certification.

Self Test

Matching

1. ____ MIS director/CIO
2. ____ Data communications analysts
3. ____ Network (LAN) administrator
4. ____ Application programmer
5. ____ Technical writer
6. ____ Systems analyst
7. ____ Network security specialist
8. ____ Quality assurance specialist
9. ____ System programmer
10. ____ Help desk specialist

a. evaluates, installs, and monitors data and/or voice communications equipment and software

b. analyzes user requirements to design and develop new hardware and software systems

c. writes the instructions necessary to process data into information

d. installs and maintains local area networks; identifies and resolves connectivity issues

e. solves questions about hardware, software, or telecommunications systems

f. configures routers and firewalls; specifies Web protocols and enterprise technologies

g. installs and maintains operation system software and provides technical support

h. converts the system design into the appropriate computer language

i. copyrighted software provided by an individual or company at no cost

j. works with analysts, programmers, and users to create system documentation and user materials

k. reviews programs and documentation to ensure they meet an organization's standards

l. directs a company's information service and communications functions

True/False

____ 1. Nearly 20 percent of the U.S. information technology careers — or 800,000 jobs — are open today.

____ 2. Computer equipment manufacturers include such companies as Adobe Systems, Novell, Macromedia, and Microsoft.

____ 3. In a typical IT department, the management group is responsible for analyzing, designing, developing, and implementing new information technology and maintaining and improving existing systems.

____ 4. Companies usually pay sales representatives based on the amount of product they sell.

____ 5. According to the U.S. Bureau of Labor Statistics, the slowest growing computer jobs through the year 2008 will be computer engineer, computer support specialist, systems analyst, and database administrator.

____ 6. In four-year computer information systems (CIS) degrees, students work for and receive an Applied Associate in Science (A.A.S.) degree with an emphasis in application programming.

____ 7. Trade schools offer programs primarily in the areas of programming and maintenance.

____ 8. Computing professionals typically obtain a certification by passing an examination.

____ 9. Professional organizations, such as the Institute for Certification of Computer Professionals (ICCP), establish standards to raise the competence level for the computer industry.

____ 10. Most certification tests are in an essay-question format.

Multiple Choice

____ 1. In the computer software industry, what job title designs, writes, and tests computer programs?
   a. programmer/analyst
   b. project engineer
   c. software engineer
   d. system programmer

____ 2. In the Internet industry, what job title oversees Web site performance and maintains the link between a company's Web server and ISP?
   a. Web administrator
   b. Web developer
   c. Web graphic designer
   d. Web programmer

____ 3. What job title is part of the operations group in a typical IT department?
   a. project manager
   b. computer operator
   c. project leader
   d. computer science engineer/software engineer

____ 4. What job title is *not* part of the technical services group in a typical IT department?
   a. database analyst/data modeler
   b. desktop publishing specialist
   c. computer technician/computer service technician
   d. graphic designer/illustrator

____ 5. What challenging job is ideally suited for individuals who like to troubleshoot and solve problems and have a strong background in electronics?
   a. computer education and training
   b. sales representative
   c. consultant
   d. service and repair technician

____ 6. After two years of study, what degree do students in computer information systems (CIS) programs often receive?
   a. Ph.D. or M.B.A.
   b. M.B.A. or M.S.
   c. B.S. or M.S.
   d. A.A.S. or A.S.

____ 7. What benefits are offered by both the ACM (Association for Computing Machinery) and the AITP (Association of Information Technology Professionals)?
   a. workshops, seminars, and conventions
   b. Special Interest Groups (SIGs) that bring together members
   c. programs to help with continuing education needs
   d. all of the above

____ 8. The Red Hat Certified Engineer (RHCE) program validates mastery of what operating system?
   a. UNIX
   b. Windows
   c. Linux
   d. all of the above

____ 9. How much do holders of MCSE (Microsoft Certified System Engineer), CCIE (Cisco Certified Internetworking Expert), and CNE (Certified Novell Engineer) certifications typically earn?
   a. between $6,000 and $8,000
   b. between $60,000 and $80,000
   c. between $600,000 and $800,000
   d. between $6,000,000 and $8,000,000

____ 10. When preparing for computer certification, which of the following is true?
   a. most people prefer to use a combination of self-study, online training classes, and instructor-led training
   b. most certification programs require academic coursework and are not determined by test results
   c. most professionals have the experience and skill to take a certification exam without preparation
   d. all of the above

Fill in the Blanks

1. A(n) ____________________ draws upon his or her experience to give advice to others.
2. A(n) ____________________ ensures that transfers from a community college to a college or university will receive credit for the courses already taken.
3. The ____________________ is a scientific and educational organization dedicated to advancing information technology.
4. The ____________________ is a professional association of programmers, systems analysts, and information processing managers.
5. A(n) ____________________ is a collection of people with common computer equipment or software interests that meets regularly to share information.
6. ____________________, one of the larger technology trade shows in the world, brings together more than 2,100 vendors and 200,000 attendees.
7. ____________________ ensures quality and workmanship standards and is one way companies can help to ensure that their workforce remains up to date on computers and technology.
8. Certification ____________________ include computer hardware and software vendors, independent training companies, and professional organizations.
9. Some vendor-sponsored certifications offer access to ____________________ — those still in the testing stage — and early releases.
10. A technique known as ____________________ analyzes a person's responses while taking a certification test.

Complete the Table

COMPUTER INDUSTRY DISCIPLINE DIFFERENCES

____________________ ____________________	**Computer Science/ Software Engineering**	____________________ ____________________
Practical and application oriented	____________________	Design oriented
____________________ ____________________	Mathematics and science oriented	____________________ ____________________
Understanding how to design and implement information systems	____________________ ____________________ ____________________	Understanding the fundamental nature of hardware
Degrees include __________ ____________________	Degrees include B.S., M.S., Ph.D.	Degrees include __________ ____________________

Things to Think About

1. How is the computer equipment industry similar to and different from the computer software industry? Can a person be successful in one industry without knowledge of the other? Why or why not?
2. Are salaries for job titles in a typical IT department (see Figure 16-7 on page 16.09) commensurate with the education, skills, talent, and experience required? Why or why not?
3. What skills must people in computer education and training, sales, service and repair, and consulting share? What skills are unique to an area?
4. How do employees, employers, customers, and the computer industry benefit from certification? What group benefits most? Why?

Puzzle

All of the words described below appear in the puzzle. Words may be either forward or backward, across, up and down, or diagonal. Circle each word as you find it.

Computer Careers and Certification

```
                          C
                        P O A
                      W S N R S
                    R Z I S T R L
                  H D X R U I T E O
                W E I S O L C Q N T O
              E C L S Y T T U B O E S H
            B U O P R S A A L S I C T A C
          M U S M D E T R N A P T H C S C S
        A I O E P E E E T T T R A N U I U B E
      S V S O R U S N M S S I O C I D A E X E D
    T U P D N G T K I P I O O J I C O M D E X W A
  E E O W I C R E S G R N F N E F A R Q X H M Y R R
R E M M A R G O R P N O I T A C I L P P A F Q S P P T
  E J C T E Z U O E E G M W G T T W A A W I P R R S
    M R P C C P P C T R D A R M R R T R X O E O Y
      M R T C H E I C A A R E A E I E W N P J L
        A O A S R A E M B E E N C T B S O E A
          R G D A L J M E E M A + E O L C N
            G C T I O E W N E G A R E T A
              O O S R R X G N E S V L S
                R T P M A I T R E E M
                  P I C K N O D A E
                    B S L E B D T
                      E P E E S
                        W R Y
                          S
```

Analyzes software requirements and designs software solutions

Develops system software

Oversees Web site performance

Analyzes, designs, implements, and supports Web applications

Supports a company's Internet strategy

Creates and develops Webcasts featuring streaming rich media

Maintains an organization's Web site

Directs a company's information service and communications functions

Coordinates projects; performs systems analysis and programming tasks

Oversees all assigned projects

Performs equipment-related activities

Converts the system design into the appropriate computer language

Works with analysts, programmers, and users to create system documentation

Designs and develops new hardware and software systems

Installs and maintains operating system software

Solves procedural and software questions

Draws upon his or her experience to give advice to others

Academic program that emphasizes the practical aspects of computing

Ensures that student transfers receive credit for courses taken

Academic program that stresses the theoretical side of programming

Academic program that teaches design and development of computer components

Offer programs primarily in the areas of programming and maintenance

Scientific and educational organization dedicated to advancing IT

Collection of people with similar computer equipment or software interests

One of the larger technology trade shows

Ensures a level of competency, skills, or quality in a particular area

Companies that develop and administer certification

Certification program that validates mastery of the Linux operating system

Certification program designed to measure skills with areas of Microsoft Office

Certification program that validates knowledge of Microsoft operating systems

One of seven certification tracks in the MCP Program

Certification that show understanding of the computer as a business tool

Certification that affirms competency of computer repair technicians

Certifies that an individual is qualified to work with Internetworking technologies

Certification that demonstrates in-depth knowledge of the Novell network system

Internet certification that targets professionals who provide Web presence security

Computer products still in the testing stage

Analyzes a person's responses while he or she is taking a test

Self Test Answers

Matching	True/False	Multiple Choice
1. *l* [p. 16.09]	1. *T* [p. 16.02]	1. *a* [p. 16.06]
2. *a* [p. 16.09]	2. *F* [p. 16.04]	2. *a* [p. 16.07]
3. *d* [p. 16.09]	3. *F* [p. 16.08]	3. *b* [p. 16.09]
4. *h* [p. 16.09]	4. *T* [p. 16.10]	4. *c* [p. 16.09]
5. *j* [p. 16.09]	5. *F* [p. 16.11]	5. *d* [p. 16.10]
6. *b* [p. 16.09]	6. *F* [p. 16.12]	6. *d* [p. 16.12]
7. *f* [p. 16.09]	7. *T* [p. 16.13]	7. *d* [p. 16.14]
8. *k* [p. 16.09]	8. *T* [p. 16.16]	8. *c* [p. 16.18]
9. *g* [p. 16.09]	9. *T* [p. 16.26]	9. *b* [p. 16.20]
10. *e* [p. 16.09]	10. *F* [p. 16.29]	10. *a* [p. 16.28]

Fill in the Blanks

1. *consultant* [p. 16.11]
2. *articulation agreement* [p. 16.13]
3. *Association for Computing Machinery (ACM)* [p. 16.14]
4. *Association of Information Technology Professionals (AITP)* [p. 16.14]
5. *user group* [p. 16.14]
6. *COMDEX* [p. 16.14]
7. *Certification* [p. 16.16]
8. *sponsors* [p. 16.16]
9. *beta products* [p. 16.26]
10. *computerized adaptive testing (CAT)* [p. 16.30]

Complete the Table

COMPUTER INDUSTRY DISCIPLINE DIFFERENCES

Computer Information Systems	**Computer Science/ Software Engineering**	*Computer Engineering*
Practical and application oriented	*Theoretical oriented*	Design oriented
Business and management oriented	Mathematics and science oriented	*Mathematics and science oriented*
Understanding how to design and implement information systems	*Understanding the fundamental nature of software*	Understanding the fundamental nature of hardware
Degrees include *A.A.S., B.S., M.S., Ph.D.*	Degrees include B.S., M.S., Ph.D.	Degrees include *B.S., M.S., Ph.D.*

Things to Think About

Answers will vary.

Puzzle Answer

Computer Careers and Certification

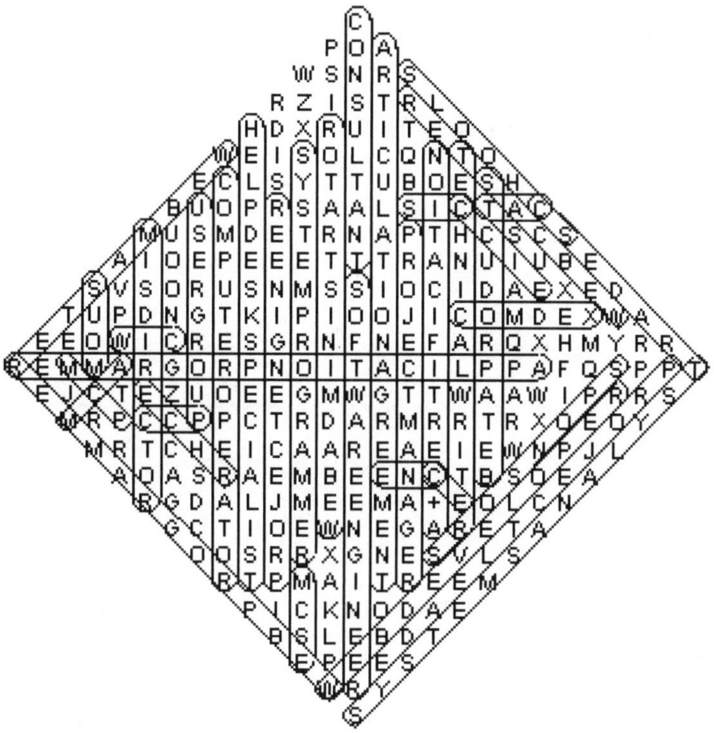

NOTES

NOTES

NOTES

NOTES

NOTES